WILLIAM MORRIS

WILLIAM MORRIS

by

HOLBROOK JACKSON

GREENWOOD PRESS, PUBLISHERS
WESTPORT, CONNECTICUT

Originally published in 1908 and 1926
by Jonathan Cape, Ltd., London

First Greenwood Reprinting 1971

Library of Congress Catalogue Card Number 79-110848

SBN 8371-4515-5

Printed in the United States of America

CONTENTS

CONTENTS

PREFACE

WHEN Messrs. Jonathan Cape invited me to prepare a new edition of my study of William Morris, I believed that no more than a few minor corrections to the edition of 1908 would have been necessary. This proved to be a miscalculation. I found that my point of view with regard to certain phases of Morris's work had changed, and in making such alterations as that circumstance demanded, my interest in the subject revived to such an extent that I found myself re-writing the book. All the old chapters have been revised and extended, and four new chapters have been added. One, 'A Portrait of William Morris,' is an attempt at a word-picture of the man as he was in his prime; another is devoted to the Kelmscott Press; a third to Morris's literary work; and in the concluding chapter I have tried to estimate his achievement in the perspective of the thirty years which have passed since his death. It is perhaps no exaggeration, therefore, to describe this study of one of the greatest and most useful men of last century, as a new book. Acknowledgment is made either in the text or in a footnote for the numerous occasions on which I have been indebted to other writers for matters of fact, but I should be lacking in courtesy if I let this opportunity pass without again expressing my indebtedness to Professor J. W. Mackail's *Life of William Morris*, which I have re-read with renewed admiration, pleasure and profit.

HOLBROOK JACKSON

7

. . . I would that the loving were loved, and I would that the weary should sleep,

And that man should hearken to man, and that he that soweth should reap.

Sigurd the Volsung

WILLIAM MORRIS

CHAPTER ONE

Early Days

*

WILLIAM MORRIS, born at Elm House, Clay Hill, Walthamstow, on 24 March, 1834, was of Welsh and English descent. His paternal grandfather was a tradesman of Worcester, who married a daughter of Dr. Charles Stanley, a naval surgeon, of Nottingham. His father was born at Worcester, and at the age of twenty-three went to London, where he entered, and afterwards became a partner in, a discount-broking house in the City. William Morris, senior, was a capable man of affairs, and his efforts within the firm, together with a successful investment in Cornish copper mines, soon made him rich. Shortly after becoming a partner he married Emma Shelton, the daughter of a Worcester family to whom the Morrises were distantly related.

The newly-married couple set up house over the business premises in Lombard Street, and here their eldest children, both daughters, were born. In 1833 they removed to Walthamstow, where William Morris, the poet and craftsman, was born. The house was within two miles of Epping Forest. It overlooked the Lea Valley, and this pleasant and distinctly English rural scene became the appropriate and agreeable setting of his earliest days. In 1840, when William was in his seventh year, the family trekked across the forest to Woodford Hall, a large

9

Georgian mansion in a park of fifty acres, on the high
road between London and Epping. Here they remained until 1848, when, on the death of the father,
the family returned to Walthamstow, living at
Water House until 1856.

Practically the whole of William Morris's youth
was thus spent amid the sylvan amenities of Epping
Forest. The beauty of its glades of pollarded hornbeam, beech and holly, and the large skies and lone
distances of the Essex lowlands, struck deep into his
nature. He was fully conscious of the charm of his
surroundings, and when, in later youth, he was at
Marlborough College his imagination always wan-
dered back to the Epping homeland.

'It is now only seven weeks to the holidays,' he
wrote to a sister in the earliest extant specimen of his
writing; 'there I go again! Just like me! always
harping on the holidays. I am sure you must think
me a great fool to be always thinking about home,
but I really can't help it. I don't think it is my fault,
for there are such a lot of things I want to do and
say and see.'[1]

The child was father to the man : there were always
so many things he wanted to do and say and see, and
few men have managed to do and say and see more
in a short life, and still fewer men of genius have had
opportunity of such orderly growth towards the full
realization of personal expression. The life of Morris was a logical sequence, constantly expanding and

[1] *Life*. Mackail, i. 18.

realizing itself like a dream. His experiences, surroundings and friendships all contributed in their
time and place to this rhythmical unfolding of a life
which after early manhood might have been curtailed
at any time but would still have seemed complete.

As a child William Morris was delicate, but he
soon gained strength in the pure air of Epping. He
was studious and retiring, and at a very early age a
devoted reader of books. Neither he nor any member
of his family knew exactly when he learnt to read;
it would seem to have been a faculty which he
acquired by instinct. At the age of four he was deep
in the Waverley Novels. By the age of seven he had
devoured Scott and most of Marryat, and Lane's
Arabian Nights had become a constant source of joy.
At an early age, also, he was impressed by colour and
form, and remembered in after life how his childish
mind had been moved by a picture of Abraham and
Isaac worked in worsted; by Indian cabinets; by a
carved ivory junk with gilded puppets; and by 'naif
gross ghost stories, read long ago in queer little
penny garlands with woodcuts.'[1] His love of the pictorial was further gratified by the quaint illustrations
in an old Gerard's *Herbal* which he found among the
books of the house. There is little cause for doubt
that the study of the pictures in this book, and an
early enthusiasm for Heraldry, determined the character of much of his later work as a decorator.

But early as he acquired the reading faculty, he did
not learn how to use a pen until much after the

[1] *Id.* i. 8.

normal age, and he never became reliable in his spelling. An instance of this orthographic incompetence occurs at the peak of his career when several sheets of *The Life and Death of Jason* had to be cancelled and reprinted owing to a mistake in the spelling of a simple word, a word so common as to have convinced the printer's reader that Morris's version was intentional.

Up to the age of nine William Morris received no education save an occasional lesson from his sister's governess. Later he was sent to a 'preparatory school for young gentlemen,' kept by two ladies, at first in Walthamstow, Morris riding backwards and forwards on his pony, and then at Woodford. In 1848, when he was just under fourteen, he entered Marlborough College, then newly established, and remained there until 1851. In these early years the college was in a state of chaos, there was little organization, insufficient accommodation and funds, and building operations were proceeding all the time.

The educational system was bad even for those days, but this was of little importance to a boy of the type of Morris; perhaps it was an advantage. His real education went on apart from system. He found the materials in Savernake Forest and on the Downs; in the ancient barrows of Silbury and Pewsey; in the stone circles of Avebury and the Roman Villa at Kennet; in the ancient churches of the district and in the college library, which was fortunately well provided with works on archæology and ecclesiastical architecture. In after years he used to say that he left

Marlborough 'a good archæologist, and knowing most of what there was to be known about English Gothic.'[1] And this was the basis of many of his future activities. His archaism was never a pose, as it came to be with some of his followers; it was an innate preference. He threw-back instinctively to an early period and later in life found reasons for doing so in his effort to restore sane and organic design in craftsmanship and the decorative arts.

The childhood and youth of William Morris were a continuous romance; not a romance of actual deeds, but of coloured dreams. The joys of knight errantry were his as he raced about Woodford Hall upon his pony clad in a suit of toy armour. Wherever he was he recreated his surroundings out of his own visions. He roamed over Epping and Savernake, pondering deeply upon the life of their beautiful glades, giving them for himself and for those who then had his confidence, and for those who have since read his books, a new significance. The backgrounds of several of his romances are records of the impressions of these experiences. Throughout the whole of his life his education (for it never ended) was thus acquired, haphazard it might seem, but by those chances which Anatole France has attributed in the last resort to God. He disliked impressionism as such, but more than most artists he was the product of the external impressions of certain things and scenes selected by the unerring intuitions of genius. His pastors and masters had little to do with the evolution of his

[1] *Life*. Mackail, i. 16.

genius. His home life was agreeable because it was spacious and free: it left room for him to grow. He confessed to Wilfrid Scawen Blount during the last weeks of his life that neither his parents nor any of his relations had the least idea of beauty. The beauty sense he had acquired 'naturally.'

'I remember as a boy,' he said, 'going into Canterbury Cathedral and thinking that the gates of heaven had been opened to me, also when I first saw an illuminated manuscript. These first pleasures which I discovered for myself were stronger than anything else I have had in life.'[1]

Morris discovered things for himself; his life was an adventure of discoveries. At school he was not noted for sport, nor, in the ordinary way, for study. Here again he was fortunate. Marlborough had not yet been caught by the sports mania, and its *laisser faire* educational method, however bad for others, was his opportunity. He thus played his own game of life and hammered out his own intellectual destiny. He was not incapable of study so long as the subject squared with his inner needs. Certain subjects were, of course, anathema; arithmetic, for instance, and Latin; he preferred English history to Greek, showing once again the child as father of the man. He had a violent temper, and was thought a little mad by his schoolfellows, who, nevertheless, were not averse from listening to his endless stories about knights and fairies. He had the usual boyish

[1] *My Diaries.* Blount, i. 229.

enthusiasm for silkworms and birds' eggs; but his outstanding taste was for books and the beauties of Nature in their more picturesque aspects. He was, in short, a born romantic, but even in these young days the intense activity of hand and brain, which so characterized his whole life, began to show itself. It is recorded how his fingers must ever be handling something, as though the craftsman in him already sought but could not yet find expression. A story is told of how he found relief from this restlessness by endless net-making: 'With one end of the net fastened to a desk in the big schoolroom he would work at it for hours together, his fingers moving almost automatically.'[1] This again was in character, for as we shall presently discover, his romanticism was to take a novel turn; it was to leave the realm of faery, and apply itself to the hard facts of life; to divert the sense of wonder and the passion for beauty into the making of beautiful things which eventually were to become the starting-points for the wonderland of a new civilization: in a phrase – the discovery of the romance of work. Carlyle had asserted the duty of work, and more than one philosopher, economist and moralist had expounded its necessity; it was for Morris to reveal its romance.

It was decided that he should study for the Church, and, after leaving Marlborough, he read at home with a private tutor until he was able to go up to Oxford for matriculation. The trend of his mind and imagination at this time, his love not only of

[1] *Life*. Mackail, i. 17.

medieval architecture, old churches and church music, but of the cloistered life of the Middle Ages, pointed to the Church as a natural vocation. His tutor, the Rev. F. B. Guy, afterwards a Canon of St. Alban's, was a man of similar tastes and sympathies, and he played an important part in helping the poet to discover himself. Morris went up to Oxford in June, 1852, and matriculated at Exeter College. On the very threshold of the Oxford life which was to have so profound an influence on his career, the star which watched over the progression of his genius was in the ascendant; for it was during the examination in the Hall of Exeter that he first met Edward Burne-Jones, who was to become his life-long friend and co-worker in the realization of a dream of art which opened, perhaps for the last time, a magic casement through which those of our bewildered and machine-menaced age who cared, might contemplate, not a fairy land forlorn, but a happy world of inspiring work and gracious leisure, and thus contemplating, so the dreamers dreamed, be moved to recapture somewhat of that beautiful vision for themselves and those who would come after them.

CHAPTER TWO

The Inspiration of Oxford

*

WILLIAM MORRIS entered into residence at Exeter College in 1853, and took his Bachelor's degree in 1856; it was during these three years that the curve of his future life was determined. Oxford, of all cities, 'so venerable, so lovely, so unravaged by the fierce intellectual life of our century,' was the one most likely to develop such a character as his. Oxford still 'whispering from her towers the last enchantments' of those Middle Ages where he had dwelt as in a dream was now as a dream come true. He revelled among her lawns and libraries, her grey and gracious architecture and immemorial traditions, feeding his imagination with just those realities which it craved. And the new-found fellowship with Edward Burne-Jones, destined to grow into so memorable a friendship, gave him for the first time a full and intimate companionship in tastes and ideals.

The moment also was propitious, for the intellectual atmosphere was beginning to thrill with one of those periodical awakenings which rarely leave Oxford unmoved. The Tractarian movement still echoed through the quadrangles, and although past its heyday, its reverberations were to be heard in the new impulsion towards art then finding expression in that romantic renaissance which was soon to be known as the special province of the pre-Raphaelite Brotherhood. He had for long been familiar with the work of Tennyson, and though more critical of the then new poet than were others of his set, his attitude in Canon Dixon's words was 'defiant admiration.'[1] He must have found many affinities in the 'Lady of Shalott' and the 'Palace of Art'; and it was not long before he was to find personal as well as artistic intimacy with Rossetti, Swinburne and Meredith. But the most powerful influence was Ruskin. He had read with sympathy the early volumes of *Modern Painters* and sympathy became enthusiasm with the reading of the *Seven Lamps of Architecture.*[2]

But the ideas to which he was introduced by these books were to be augmented and turned into something like a religion for him by the time the three volumes of *The Stones of Venice* had been published, in the years 1851–3. The famous chapter called 'The Nature of Gothic' became a bible for him, and years afterwards he reverently printed it on the Kelmscott Press. The teachings of Charles Kingsley, Frederick Denison Maurice and Carlyle, also played their part in focussing his outlook upon social conditions, particularly the last writer whose *Past and Present* went far towards making him a convinced enemy of competitive commerce. But with the exception of 'The Nature of Gothic,' no literary work held Morris so firmly or meant so much to him, both then and afterwards, as Chaucer's *Canterbury Tales*

[1] *Life.* Mackail, i. 45.
[2] 'Ruskin . . . before my days of practical Socialism, was my master towards the ideal . . . and, looking backward, I cannot help saying, by the way, how deadly dull the world would have been twenty years ago but for Ruskin.' *How I became a Socialist.* William Morris (1896).

and Malory's *Morte d'Arthur*. Chaucer was his ac-
knowledged master in song, as Malory was in prose,
whilst the pilgrims of Canterbury and the knights of
Avalon were the dream companions of all his days;
and Chaucer's England was his spiritual home at all
times. The Prologue to *The Earthly Paradise* (1868)
enjoins the reader to

Forget six counties overhung with smoke,
Forget the snorting steam and piston stroke,
Forget the spreading of the hideous town;
Think rather of the pack-horse on the down,
And dream of London, small, and white, and clean,
The clear Thames bordered by its gardens green . . .

where Geoffrey Chaucer 'nigh the thronged wharf'
plies his pen over bills of lading of

Florence gold cloth, and Ypres napery
And cloth of Bruges, and hogsheads of Guienne.

This England, once more clean and white and green,
was the scenario of *News from Nowhere* (1891), and
his last tribute to his Master and his Master's England was the *magnum opus* of the Kelmscott Press
completed the year Morris died.

Burne-Jones and Morris, so far as their own college was concerned, lived very much to themselves.
But Burne-Jones had a circle of Birmingham friends
at Pembroke College. Morris became one of this
group of ardent souls, which included William Fulford, Cormell Price, Harry Macdonald, and Richard
Watson (afterwards Canon) Dixon. They came to be

known among themselves as the Set, and later on as
the Brotherhood. Their aim at first was the application of religious and philosophical ideas to life, and
there was serious talk of Morris founding and en-
dowing a monastery wherein they might give expression to their ideals, which were mainly derived from
Ruskin, Carlyle and Tennyson.

But this desire never developed, because Morris
became conscious of that love of art, always latent,
which eventually determined the true course of his
life. On his coming of age he inherited a fortune of
nearly £1,000 a year. At this time he was still intent
upon Holy Orders. The discovery that he could
better express his mission in life by weaving his
imagination into works of art came later and gradually. Nor at this period was there any outward indi-
cation of the democratic faith which inspired his later
activities. If he was anything very definite he was,
as in some measure he always remained, a benevolent
despot, an aristocrat with monastic and humane
impulses.

He was healthy in body, and tireless in the work he
loved; busy with modern ideas and ancient studies,
particularly of medieval times; playful, buoyant and
robust, with an amazing amount of special knowledge upon the subjects which interested him, and
abundant enthusiasm for everything he undertook
and for all his interests both practical and visionary.
He lived with gusto, and for all his medievalism,
laughed and rollicked through his days like a young
Titan on a Bank Holiday.

There are two contemporary descriptions of him. The earlier is by Burne-Jones:

'From the first I knew how different he was from all the men I had ever met,' he says; 'he talked with vehemence, and sometimes with violence. I never knew him languid or tired. He was slight in figure in those days; his hair was dark brown and very thick, his nose straight, his eyes hazel-coloured, his mouth exceedingly delicate and beautiful.'[1]

This portrait is confirmed by Canon Dixon, writing a year or two later:

'At this time, Morris was an aristocrat, and a High Churchman. His manners and tastes and sympathies were all aristocratic. His countenance was beautiful in features and expression, particularly in the expression of purity. Occasionally it had a melancholy look. He had a finely-cut mouth, the short upper-lip adding greatly to the purity of expression. I have a vivid recollection of the splendid beauty of his expression at this time.'[2]

In 1854 he visited Belgium and Northern France. On this journey he made the acquaintance of some of the finest examples of northern Gothic, and the impression made upon him by the churches of Amiens, Beauvais and Chartres was profound and lasting. The following year Morris, Burne-Jones and Fulford went on a walking tour through Normandy, revisiting memorable places and making new

[1] *Life*. Mackail, i. 35.   [2] *Id*. i. 46.

acquaintances among the distinguished architectural works of that country. But this journey was memorable for another reason. The talks and impressions of the tour found expression on the return journey in the decision of Morris and Burne-Jones to abandon all ideas of taking Holy Orders and henceforth definitely to devote their lives to art. They arrived at this conclusion one August night on the quay at Havre. Burne-Jones was to be a painter, Morris an architect. The circumstances attending this important decision have been described by the former. The friends had visited Paris, expending most of their time in the Church of Notre Dame; from thence, wrote Burne-Jones, we

'made northwards for Rouen, travelling gently and stopping at every Church we could find. Rouen was still a beautiful medieval city, and we stayed awhile and had our hearts filled. From there we walked to Caudebec, then by diligence to Havre, on our way to the churches of the Calvados: and it was while walking on the quay at Havre at night that we resolved definitely that we would begin a life of art, and put off our decision no longer – he should be an architect and I a painter. It was a resolve only needing final conclusion; we were bent on that road for the whole past year, and after that night's talk we never hesitated more. That was the most memorable night of my life.'[1]

Before the tour, however, Morris had discovered

[1] *Memorials of Edward Burne-Jones.* By G. B.-J., i. 114–115.

that he could write. In the winter of 1854 he read
to Burne-Jones his first poem.

'One night,' writes Canon Dixon, 'Crom Price and
I went to Exeter, and found him with Burne-Jones.
As soon as we entered the room, Burne-Jones ex-
claimed wildly, "He's a big poet!" "Who is?" asked
we. "Why, Topsy." '¹

This was the name, sometimes shortened to 'Top,'
which had been given him because of his wild curly
hair. There and then Morris was made to sit down
and read to them his first poem; it was called 'The
Willow and the Red Cliff.' His friends were full of
enthusiasm, as well they might have been. 'Well,'
said Morris, 'if this is poetry, it is very easy to write.'
And for some time afterwards he presented his friend
with a new poem almost daily. This facility for the
writing of poetry continued throughout his life.
Charles Faulkner told Birkbeck Hill that on one day
Morris had written 'seven hundred lines of *Jason*,'²
and this facility put Rossetti in a friendly rage, for in
little over Morris's first poetic year he had 'already
enough poetry for a big book,'³ and most of it would
have passed the critical test of the elder bard. Later,
he found out that he could write prose, and he wrote
those prose romances which are unsurpassed in our
language for their luxuriant beauty of phrase, magic

¹ *Life*. Mackail, i. 51.   ² *Letters of Dante Gabriel Rossetti to
William Allingham*, 1854–1870. Ed. by George Birkbeck Hill,
201.   ³ *Id*. 192–3.

of imagery, and unique knowledge of medieval archæology.

The Brotherhood had long wanted a medium for the expression of its aspirations, so with the financial aid of Morris and the intellectual co-operation of kindred spirits at Cambridge as well as Oxford, *The Oxford and Cambridge Magazine* was founded in 1856, with Morris as editor, a position he yielded to Fulford before the second number appeared. Twelve monthly numbers in all were printed, when decreasing circulation forced them to discontinue publication. *The Oxford and Cambridge Magazine*, however, stands with the Pre-Raphaelite magazine, *The Germ*, as one of the most notable products of a new era in English literature. In its pages not only appeared the earliest work of Morris, but three poems by Dante Gabriel Rossetti, whom Morris had recently met and whose work he instantly understood and liked.

Indeed, the final incident which confirmed Morris and Burne-Jones in their decision to become artists, came through the latter's introduction to Rossetti at about this time. Both of them, like most people who came within his sphere, fell under the spell of Rossetti's powerful and unique personality. Rossetti imposed a quality on the art of Burne-Jones which it never lost, and he eventually drew Morris away from architecture as a profession, and set him painting pictures. Morris articled himself to the architect Street, and entered his office in Beaumont Street, Oxford, in January, 1856. There he met Philip Webb, who became a life-long friend and, through

this connection, he came to know that other great
architect, Norman Shaw. It was these three men who
brought about the modern renaissance of domestic
architecture in England. Though Morris abandoned architecture as a profession, the master-craft
remained the keystone of his ideas about life and art;
and although Rossetti's powerful influence dominated him for a time, his career as a professional
painter was of short duration. Among modern influences Rossetti also played his part in determining
the early character of Morris's poetry. To the Oxford
group which had for its literary nucleus *The Oxford
and Cambridge Magazine*, Rossetti was little less than
a god. But at that time he, Rossetti, was inclined to
give painting precedence over poetry:

'It was a theory of his, expounded with copiousness
and vehement conviction, that English poetry was
fast reaching the termination of its long and splendid
career, and that Keats represented its final achievement. English painting, on the other hand, he regarded as in its dawn.'[1]

At the same time he was one of the first to recognize that Morris was an authentic poet. As early as
1856 he wrote to William Allingham that 'besides
writing those capital tales,' Morris 'writes poems
which are really better than the tales.'[2]

[1] *Life.* Mackail, i. 110.   [2] *Letters of Dante Gabriel Rossetti
to William Allingham*, 1854–1870. Ed. by George Birkbeck
Hill, 192.

CHAPTER THREE

The Evolution of a Craftsman

★

MORRIS abandoned his career as an architect within a year. By this time he had settled with Burne-Jones in London, whither Street had removed from Oxford. In 1857 the two friends took the rooms at 17 Red Lion Square which had been occupied by Rossetti and Deverell in the earliest days of the Pre-Raphaelite movement, and this was to be their home until the spring of 1859. Morris had before this been drawn towards designing, and it was his early skill in that art and his love of the craft-work of the Middle Ages, coupled with the necessity of having to furnish his own rooms, that his life as the re-volutionist of taste in domestic furniture began. The crafts of cabinet-making and upholstery had become so degraded that Morris could actually buy noth-ing to satisfy his taste; thus his practical genius came naturally into play. He had what furniture he wanted made to his own designs. To the rooms in Red Lion Square came Rossetti, and in his com-manding and irresistible way added his own influ-ence to that of Morris and Burne-Jones in the decoration of the furniture. The first step in the revolution of the decorative arts was thus the joint act of three outstanding geniuses – Edward Burne-Jones, Dante Gabriel Rossetti and William Morris.

Morris now turned to painting and designing with his accustomed ardour.

'Morris,' wrote Rossetti to William Allingham in 1856, 'means to become an architect, and to that end has set about becoming a painter, at which he is making progress. In all illumination and work of that kind he is quite unrivalled by anything modern that I know – Ruskin says, better than anything ancient.'[1]

In 1857 he painted his first picture. It was a subject in oils taken from the *Morte d'Arthur*; and in the same year he did his first and only picture in water-colour, whilst staying with Dixon at Manchester. In this year also Morris joined Rossetti in that high-spirited but ill-considered scheme for the decoration of the ceiling of the then new debating hall (now the library) of the Union Society at Oxford. Rooms were taken at Oxford, and the old friends of the Brotherhood pressed into the service. Rossetti had also secured the help of Burne-Jones, Arthur Hughes, Spencer Stanhope, Val Prinsep, and Hungerford Pollen. After the decoration of the Hall was finished, Morris remained at Oxford in rooms at 17 George Street, where the painters and their friends had spent many happy hours during their disinterested work of artistry.

Some of the happiest days of his life were spent in London during the few months preceding the painting of the Union Hall ceiling. He was one of the Rossetti circle, which included all that was vital and capable in the art of the period, coupled with enthusiasm and a picturesque Bohemianism. In 1858 he painted 'Queen Guenevere,' the only completed

[1] *Letters of Dante Gabriel Rossetti to William Allingham,* 1854–1870. Ed. by George Birkbeck Hill, 193–194.

painting of his now known to be extant; and in the
early months of the year his first volume of poems,
The Defence of Guenevere, appeared. His stay in
Oxford, however, caused a break with this circle,
although he paid London periodical visits, and he
visited France twice that year, once with Faulkner
and Webb in August, rowing down the Seine from
Paris, in a boat taken over from Oxford, and on
another occasion alone to buy manuscripts, armour,
ironwork, and enamels. But all this time, although
he painted diligently, his mind dwelt upon other
things. He was gradually realizing that the pursuit
of a single art was not for him. The idea of the
relationship of all the arts in the building, not only
of houses beautiful but of cities beautiful, was
clamouring for expression. The real William Morris
was nearing completion.

His stay in Oxford at this time was probably not
entirely disinterested. In the long vacation of 1857
Rossetti and Burne-Jones had become acquainted
with a lady, one of the daughters of Mr. Robert
Burden, of Oxford, whose remarkable beauty so
strongly resembled the type now familiar to everybody through Rossetti's pictures, that the young
painters persuaded her to sit to them. She attracted
William Morris in another way, and on 26 April,
1859, he and Jane Burden were married at the
parish church of St. Michael, Oxford. The ceremony was performed by Dixon, at this time curate
of St. Mary's, Lambeth, with Faulkner as best man,
and Burne-Jones and other friends as supporters.

This proved to be the closing event in the life of
the Oxford Brotherhood.

William Morris and his wife settled in furnished
rooms at 41 Great Ormond Street, London, during
the building of their new house at Upton, in Kent.
The need of a new home and the opportunity of
making the occasion a further experiment in the
realization of cherished ideas of art and life, was
not only a turning-point in his own career, but
the turning-point in the history of English domestic architecture. For just as he had found it difficult, in fact, impossible, to furnish rooms from
the commercial products of the shops, he found
it doubly impossible to build and furnish a complete house to his taste by ordinary methods.
His deepening realization of the essential relationship between architecture and the decorative arts
impelled him to try the momentous experiment of
putting his ideas into practice.

The house, called the Red House, was duly built
by Philip Webb. It was an L-shaped building of
two stories, with a high-pitched roof of red tiles,
'thus violating all the contemporary canons of
squareness, stucco, and slate.' The decorations were
the work of Morris and his friends, and most of
the furniture was designed by Webb and specially
made under his instructions. The Morrises entered
into occupation of the house in 1860, with the
full intention of making it their permanent home,
but for reasons of health they were forced to
leave the Red House after five happy years. It

was here that their two children, both girls, were born.

The building of the Red House was momentous for the problems of decoration and furnishing it raised, coupled with Morris's deepening interest in craftsmanship, ultimately resulted in the foundation of the firm of Morris and Co, whose products were to inaugurate a renaissance as well as a revolution in domestic design. The original members of the firm were William Morris, Philip Webb, C. J. Faulkner, Ford Madox Brown, Burne-Jones, Rossetti, P. P. Marshall, a surveyor and sanitary engineer, and Arthur Hughes, who withdrew from the company before it was registered. Premises were taken at No. 8 Red Lion Square, near to rooms he shared with Burne-Jones, and business started in April, 1861, under the title of Morris, Marshall, Faulkner, and Co., with a capital of one hundred pounds, borrowed from Mrs. Morris the elder, and a call of one pound per share from each member of the company.

The object of the firm was to make and supply everything that was needed in the decoration and furnishing of a house, but in the early days of its existence more attention was paid to ecclesiastical decoration. In this object the immense energy of Morris had for the first time full play, and he rapidly developed into a complete craftsman, who could turn his hand with masterly effect to any branch of the work required. As time passed the initiative of the firm devolved increasingly upon him and, with the gradual secession of the partners, the business came entirely into his hands. In 1865, when the Morrises were forced to give up the Red House, they lived at 26 Queen Square, and to this house, for the sake of convenience and economy, the business was ultimately removed. Later, a show-room in Oxford Street was opened, and finally a workshop at Merton Abbey.

In 1871, by a happy chance, he was able to take a beautiful house on a backwater of the Upper Thames, which was to be his beloved country home for the remainder of his life. He had been living with growing discontent in Bloomsbury, when he came across an advertisement in an estate agent's list announcing that Kelmscott Manor House was for sale. It was such a house as must have occupied his dreams, and its purchase is one more instance of the dream which governed his life coming true.

The grey old manor house lies on a little stream at the end of the remote and ancient village of Kelmscott, in Oxfordshire, some three miles by field-path and winding cart-road from Lechlade. Kelmscott Manor House is an irregular cluster of grey gables, with mullioned and small-leaded windows and tiled roofs of the same colour as the buildings, the tiles beautifully graded like the scales of a fish, and overgrown with golden lichen, blending wonderfully with the varied greens of the creepers, the trees, and the great dark yew hedge which dominates the gardens. Morris loved this old house, which went so well with his life and ideals, and he has recorded his affection in the penultimate chapter of *News from Nowhere*.

It was most surely his own emotions remembered in tranquillity which prompted these tender words:

'We crossed the road, and again almost without my will my hand raised the latch of a door in the wall, and we stood presently on a stone path which led up to the old house. . . . My companion gave a sigh of pleased surprise and enjoyment, nor did I wonder, for the garden between the wall and the house was redolent of the June flowers, and the roses were rolling over one another with that delicious superabundance of small well-tended gardens which at first sight takes away all thought from the beholder save that of beauty. The blackbirds were singing their loudest, the doves were cooing on the roof-ridge, the rooks in the high elm-trees beyond were garrulous among the young leaves, and the swifts wheeled whirring about the gables. And the house itself was a fit guardian for all the beauty of this heart of summer.'[1]

Here in this Thames backwater, forgotten of time and turmoil, was the embodiment of all he loved in art and life. Kelmscott became the symbol of his social religion; the centre of his Utopia.

He saw little of Kelmscott during the first year of his tenancy, which was jointly held by him and

[1] *News from Nowhere*, 1890, 226–227.

Dante Gabriel Rossetti. The previous year he had
finished *The Earthly Paradise*, and he had been
waiting to get this off his hands before taking a long-
contemplated trip to Iceland. Next to his love of the
half-forgotten lore and the less than half-remembered
crafts of the Middle Ages; the ancient buildings
and memory haunted countryside of Southern
England and Northern France, there was nothing
which attracted him more completely than the *Sagas*
of Scandinavia and the tales of the Niblungs. The
proposed journey to Iceland filled him with boyish
delight, and it is recounted by the children of Burne-
Jones how he came one day and practised the life of
a backwoodsman by building in their garden a stove
of loose bricks over which he cooked a stew. He
and three friends, including Eiríkr Magnússon, who
afterwards collaborated with him in translating the
Icelandic *Sagas*, left for Iceland in July, 1871, and
he arrived back in England towards the end of
September. A second journey to Iceland was made
in 1873.

The next few years were occupied with the business of 'the firm,' and with translations of the smaller
Icelandic *Sagas* and the *Æneids* of Virgil, with the
writing of *Love is Enough* and *Sigurd the Volsung*, and
with the craft of writing and decorating books on
vellum. Of these he produced many beautiful
examples, including copies of some of his own poems
and translations, and Fitzgerald's version of the
Rubáiyát of Omar Khayyám, of which he, with
Rossetti and Swinburne, was an early admirer. He

had taken a small house at Turnham Green, and between there and the workshops in Queen's Square and Kelmscott Manor House he spent most of his time. Besides this he found time to go down to Leek, in Staffordshire, to learn the craft of dyeing and to revive the manufacture of good and durable dyes.

Strained relations had existed for some time among the members of Morris, Marshall, Faulkner and Co., and the partnership was dissolved in March, 1875, Morris becoming the sole proprietor of the concern, which since then has been carried on under the name of Morris and Co. Constant friction had also existed between Morris and Rossetti, and the latter had finally left Kelmscott, to Morris's great relief, in the preceding summer. The attachment between these two dominant personalities was completely broken over the transactions connected with the dissolution.

William Morris had never followed, or dreamt of following, the reclusive life of the man of letters, and even less did he seek the unsecluded career of the business man. Literature for him, especially in his later years, was a by-product of a life that constantly tended towards expression and consummation in the broader current of social affairs. The firm of Morris and Co. was not a business, as that term is generally understood; it was, for Morris, a part of a social movement. His art meant nothing to him unless it bore a direct relationship with the life around him. In the broadest possible manner he was a Socialist,

and his Socialism, long before it became a conscious
political aim, found expression in the essentially
communal idea which was the basis of his demand
for a revival of handicraft. His reverence for great
architecture found expression in the Society for the
Protection of Ancient Buildings, known familiarly
as the 'anti-scrape,' which he founded in 1877, for
the purpose of rescuing the glories of the master
builders of the past from the fatal attentions of well-
meaning restorers.

In 1878 he acquired the old Georgian house on
the Upper Mall, Hammersmith, which he renamed
Kelmscott House, after his manor house in
Oxfordshire. Most of his later activities had their
origin here. In one of the rooms he set up a loom,
where he taught himself the art of weaving in his
spare time, or rather in time borrowed from those
hours usually allotted to sleep. Morris had no
spare time, he lived too fully for that, so he taught
himself weaving in the early hours of the morning
whilst most people slept. The house was decorated
by him throughout, and many of the treasures of the
Red House here found a final resting-place. Later,
when he joined the Socialist Movement, the coach-
house was turned into a lecture hall for the use
of the Hammersmith Socialist Society, of which
he became an active member, lecturing in the
hall and taking a regular and lively part in the
discussions.

He loved to think that the broad river which
flowed past his windows was the same Thames that

lapped the meadows of his beautiful Manor House
130 miles above Hammersmith, and occasionally he
would charter a boat and take his family and some
friends by water to Kelmscott.

Morris's workshops and his public life seemed to
grow side by side. The constant addition of depart-
ments made it necessary to look for larger premises,
and these were eventually found at Merton Abbey,
in Surrey. The extension of the activities of the
firm was due to the continued difficulty of procuring
such goods or materials from commercial houses as
would satisfy his exacting demands for quality and excellence of design. In this way Morris and Co. grew
from a firm of decorators into a firm of craftsmen,
making stained glass, tapestry, carpets, embroidery,
tiles, furniture, printed cotton goods, wallpapers,
furniture velvets, and other fabrics and upholstery.
Practically the same causes drove him forth as a
lecturer. He lectured on art and handicraft and the
preservation of ancient buildings, both in London
and in many provincial towns; and in 1882 he gave
evidence before the Royal Commission on Technical
Instruction.

Still, during this period William Morris led a life
that would have been lonely had it not been so fully
concentrated upon his work and his ideas. He was
at the parting of the ways with many of his old habits
and associates. Hitherto what political activity he
had displayed was connected with the National
Liberal League, but in the early 'eighties he was
more and more drawn towards Socialism, until on

13 January, 1883, he joined the Democratic Federation, which had recently been formed for the pro-
pagation of Socialism. By a coincidence on the same
day he was unanimously elected to an Honorary
Fellowship of his Oxford College.

CHAPTER FOUR

Last Years

*

HE looked upon his acceptance of Socialism as an act of renunciation. His membership card, which was endorsed by H. H. Champion, bore the words, 'William Morris, designer.' He was henceforth a workman and not a member of the middle class. He worked hard for the Federation, lecturing all over England, contributing both literature and funds to *Justice*, its official organ; and in May, 1883, he was elected a member of its Executive Committee.

This harmony continued for two years, when differences as to policy brought about a split with H. M. Hyndman, the father of the Social Democratic movement in England. Morris formed the Socialist League in 1884 with an organ of its own, called *The Commonweal*, which he ran himself, and to which he contributed, besides other matter, *The Dream of John Ball* and *News from Nowhere*. The League prospered for several years, and in spite of many differences with his fellow-members, Morris remained a member until 1890, and he edited *The Commonweal* until he was deposed in 1889.

But some years prior to these events he had been drawn again more intimately into literature and art. In 1887 he published his translation of the *Odyssey*, and in 1889 the two first of his prose romances, *The House of the Wolfings* and *The Roots of the Mountains*. The example of his work at Merton Abbey was influencing many young artists and craftsmen, and he eventually threw his energies into the Arts and Crafts Movement, then in its infancy, and largely inspired by his enthusiasm and example. He joined the Art Worker's Guild, and afterwards the Arts and Crafts Exhibition Society, became less and less a militant Socialist, and devoted an increasing number of his lectures purely to questions of art in relation to industry and life in general.

In 1890 *The Story of the Glittering Plain* appeared in the *English Illustrated Magazine,* and *News from Nowhere* was issued in paper covers for one shilling. In the same year Morris busied himself with what was to be the final work of his active and productive life, the Kelmscott Press. His love of books found expression in the desire to produce beautiful books. He secured the co-operation of Emery Walker and T. J. Cobden-Sanderson, and designed type-faces, initials and ornaments, and by the beginning of 1891 the Kelmscott Press was established in premises on the Upper Mall, Hammersmith, just above Kelmscott House. The first book printed on the press was Morris's own *Story of the Glittering Plain.*

Almost coincidental with the establishment of the Kelmscott Press the sign of illness, which was to have a fatal termination five years later, appeared. That summer he went for a short tour in Northern France with his daughter Jenny, and in the autumn he commenced publishing his translations of the Icelandic *Sagas.* The remaining years of his life were full of the old activity. He fought for the causes he had at heart and worked unceasingly. He protested against the restorations at Peterborough Cathedral, St. Mark's, Venice, and the 'taming' of Epping Forest. Several journeys were taken to the provinces for the purpose of lecturing, and yet another trip to Northern France.

But most of the time during these last years was occupied with the Kelmscott Press. This was not only his last, but in some ways his greatest individual enthusiasm. Masterpiece after masterpiece came from the great press as his years ebbed out, and he filled in any odd moments left over from his all-absorbing work as a printer by adding to his growing list of prose romances. On the death of Tennyson, in 1892, there was a rumour that he had been approached by a member of Mr. Gladstone's Cabinet with an offer of the vacant Laureateship, and that though he was pleased with the implied honour, he had made it quite clear that he could not accept such an office.[1] He spoke a few words at the funeral of the Socialist, Sergius Stepniak, in 1894; and in January of the following year he spoke for the last time in public at a meeting of the Society for Checking the Abuses of Public Advertising.

[1] The rumour has been laid by Wilfrid Scawen Blount, who saw Morris at Hammersmith at about the time and asked him whether it was true. 'It is all a lie,' he said, 'about their having offered to make me Laureate. Bryce came to see me and talked of it, but it was only on his own private account. I was fool enough to tell Ellis, and he told his son, who must needs repeat it at the National Liberal Club, and so it go into the papers.' *My Diaries*. Wilfrid Scawen Blount, i, 82.

The two most important works of these last
months of his life were the completion of the Kelmscott *Chaucer*, which had been in process of creation
in one way and another for some five years, and a
year and nine months in actual printing; and his last
prose romance, *The Sundering Flood*. Each was
strangely typical of his life and his impending end.
His whole career was to him a practical embodiment
of the spirit of the period of Chaucer, and his poems
were, in more ways than one, a modern reflection of
the genius of the *Canterbury Pilgrims*. The *Chaucer*
was finished on 2 June, 1896, and two copies were
ready for him on his return from Sussex, where he
had been spending a few days in search of health
with his friend, Wilfrid Scawen Blount. A little
under three years before, this old friend found
Morris at Kelmscott 'in fine spirits, and inexhaustible energy;' but although the fine spirit
remained the energy proved far from inexhaustible.
He spoke of his maladies cheerfully, but Blount
found him feeble and aged, and feared the presence of some form of consumption from which
he would not recover. But in spite of it all his
spirits remained good and he talked as brilliantly
as ever.[1]

His health grew rapidly worse, and the splendid
energy of the craftsman and poet began to flag. A
voyage to the North Cape was advised and taken.
He left London on 22 July, and arrived back at
Tilbury on 18 August. The voyage had done no

[1] *Id.* i. 228–229.

good, and his one desire now was to get away to
Kelmscott. But he was never to see his beautiful
country home again. His illness took a serious turn,
and he went to Kelmscott House, Hammersmith,
where he died on the morning of Saturday, 3 October,
1896, in his sixty-third year.

On 6 October, he was buried in the little church-
yard of Kelmscott. It was a bright, windy day
following a night of storm. The roads were strewn
with leaves, and the orchards with fallen apples.
The coffin was borne from Lechlade station upon
one of the Kelmscott farm-wagons. There was no
display of mourning for this man who had lived so
eventfully and worked so well. The farm-wagon was
one of the yellow-bodied, red-wheeled vehicles of the
locality; it was wreathed with vine and willow and
carpeted with green moss, and the unpolished oak
coffin, with its handles of wrought iron, was covered
with a treasured piece of Broussa brocade, upon
which was laid a wreath of bay.

'With the family and friends were mingled
workmen from Merton Abbey and Oxford Street,
comrades of the Socialist League, pupils of the
Art Worker's Guild, and Kelmscott villagers in
their daily working dress. There was no pomp
of organized mourning, and the ceremony was of
the shortest and simplest. Among associates and
followers of later years were the few survivors of that
remarkable fellowship which had founded the Oxford
Brotherhood and the firm of Red Lion Square;

and at the head of the grave Sir Edward Burne-Jones, the closest and the first friend of all, stood and saw a great part of his own life lowered into earth.'[1]

[1] *Life.* Mackail, ii. 348–349.

CHAPTER FIVE

A Portrait of William Morris

*

WILLIAM MORRIS lived in an era of problems and he was an outstanding figure of a group of men of genius most of whom were not only centres of problems of one kind or another but were often problematical themselves. Morris was never a problem. He was as clear in personality and purpose to those who knew him either remotely or intimately that all published records of him coincide so exactly as to read like a conspiracy of benevolent plagiarism. But the charge would be absurd. The resemblance is due to the circumstance that Morris was an unusual but easily recognizable fact, namely, an inspired workman of tireless energy, profound honesty of purpose and incalculable ability. Stripped of these superlatives, which are none the less true, William Morris was first and foremost a workman of genius. He said that he was 'born out of his due time' because his age had no place for workmen of genius. He became a Socialist because he thought Socialism aimed at creating a state fit for workmen of genius to live in. He ceased to work for this ideal not because he found that the aim was otherwise, for the saving grace of Socialism is that every Socialist has his own Utopia, but because, in the first place, of differences of opinion on matters of progress towards that aim, and in the second, because he came to doubt the character and ability of the man-power enrolled for the campaign. In short, his comrades in revolt were only theoretically comrades in arms. It

was not their fault that they could not catch up to
Morris; few, if any could. It was a compliment to
his faith in his fellows that he thought they could.
So he gave up politics and got back to work, which
he had never entirely abandoned; he gave up trying
to argue an obdurate and reluctant world into
putting its house in order and once more got down
to the many-sided activities of his trade as workman
of genius.

He looked the part; to the superficial glance he
was a man of action rather than a man of thought.
Sturdy, broad-shouldered, bearded, ruddy com-
plexioned, and grey-blue-eyed; with an unruly top-
knot and otherwise tangled locks neither light nor
dark and going grey; a navy blue dusty and paint-
splashed serge suit, bright butcher-blue shirt and
soft collar to match, generally crumpled, and no
neck-tie; a rolling, busy stride, as if he had lots to do,
and there is the outward and visible William Morris
as he appeared at any time in the late 'eighties and
early 'nineties save towards the end when his hair
became white but remained tempestuous and he
walked less quickly, aided by a stick.

What manner of man looked and rolled thus
with so much energy, with such gusto, for he
exuded zest of life? He looked alive; he looked
virile, masculine, obviously a man. He was all
that and more and not even the most careless of
observers could make any mistake about it. Characteristically he enjoyed his appearance and the
impression it created. This was not pose. The

appearance was real enough, and Morris relished life
only as it filtered through himself. He was incapable
of living by proxy. One of his most enjoyable experiences was being mistaken for a shipmate by a
seafaring man. Others had noted the sea-captaincy
of his outward aspect, but his friends generally preferred to see in him something of the seaman of other
days, and they linked him up with the romantic
characters of Scandinavian myth. Morris was a
Viking *redivivus*. He doubtless liked that com-
parison also, and even acted the part a little. When
nearing his end he had a sick man's fancy for Iceland, a country he knew well and liked well, and at
about the same time when on a visit to Wilfrid
Blount's Sussex home, he growled at the fine weather,
it was Maytime.

'I am a man of the North,' he said, 'I am disappointed at the fine weather we are having here. I
had hoped it would rain, so that I could sit indoors
and watch it beating on the windows.'[1]

He liked the idea of northern hardihood, and was
never afraid of bad weather. In January, 1895,
when his health was obviously declining, he was
returning from a meeting of the Society for the
Protection of Ancient Buildings, and as he laboured
up Buckingham Street, the friend with him, noticing
his weakness, observed that it was the worst time of
the year. 'No, it ain't,' he returned, 'it's a very fine

[1] *My Diaries*. Blount, i. 229.

time of the year indeed: I'm getting old, that's what it is.'[1]

Blount also noted a striking resemblance between Morris and Magnússon, his Icelandic friend and collaborator in the Scandinavian myth translations. 'It is curious how much alike the two are physically – short, thick, sturdy men of the pale, blue-eyed type. . . .'[2]

All of which is historical and documentable and therefore true; but it is by no means the whole truth and unless Morris the Baltic sea-captain, last of the Vikings, born out of his due time, be placed in correct perspective with certain other facts and phases, we are not likely to get an all-round portrait of the real man. Looking more attentively then at this sturdy figure clad in navy blue serge rolling down Kensington High Street and being mistaken for the late captain of the *Sea Swallow*, other details of no little importance will present themselves for consideration. The blue eyes,[3] for instance, are not solely the firm, practical eyes of a captain of men, eyes which see clearly and exactly and signal swiftly to a brain capable of rapid decisions; his eyes had other qualities. Sometimes they had the faraway look of the visionary. They saw things not of this earth. They were the eyes of the dreamer of romance, but the visions he saw were never allowed to seduce him from the path of reality.

[1] *Life*. Mackail, ii. 320.   [2] *My Diaries*. Blount, i. 77.
[3] Burne-Jones said Morris's eyes were ' hazel-coloured.' See *ante*, 21.

There was a classic refinement and beauty in his features, particularly in profile, but the inner restlessness of the man was revealed in the lines on his fine brow. Burne-Jones who knew him and loved him better than any of his friends recognized and lamented the triumph of Morris's boisterous and kinetic character over his romantic background.

'He is full of enthusiasm for things holy and beautiful and true,' he said, 'and what is rarest, of the most exquisite perception and judgment in them. For myself, he has tinged my whole inner being with the beauty of his own, and I know not a single gift for which I owe such gratitude to Heaven as his friendship. If it were not for his boisterous mad outbursts and freaks, which break the romance he sheds around him – at least to me – he would be a perfect hero.'[1]

There speaks the recluse, the confirmed mystic, who would like to have kept Morris to the hieratic dreams of his youth. But it was not to be, and if Burne-Jones lost a perfect hero he gained a perfect friend, and England, a great citizen.

It was the human Morris that survived, and even that was a little inhuman when it came to his work. His gift for doing more work better than anyone else was uncanny, and he brooked no interference with this the main object of his life. 'For me to rest from work means to die,' he once said to Theodore Watts-

---

[1] *Memorials of Edward Burne-Jones,* i. 96.

Dunton. The endless netting which employed his restless fingers at Marlborough College was prophetic and symbolical of his whole life.

'When not absorbed in some occupation that he loved – and in no other would he move – his restlessness was that of a young animal. In conversation he could rarely sit still for ten consecutive minutes, but must needs spring from his seat and walk round the room, as if every limb were eager to take part in the talk.'[1]

It was a sort of intellectual coltishness; he loved to frisk, and superabundant energy forced him to frisk; his muscles went on moving even when he was externally and temporarily static. He had a muscular movement in the back peculiar to himself, Burne-Jones told Wilfrid Blount, which caused the rungs of the chair in which he happened to be sitting to fly out.[2] Burne-Jones tried to recapture some of his rare sayings, but 'somehow it always seemed flattish the day after, with all the savour gone out. There is no giving the singularity and the independence of his remarks from anything that went before,' or the manner he had of 'putting his fist out to explain a thing to you.'[3]

This boisterousness was stimulating as well as disturbing. He radiated vitality and was a certain corrective of the blue devils. In a letter to Mark

[1] *Old Familiar Faces*. Watts-Dunton, 247.
[2] *My Diaries*. Blount, i. 111.
[3] *Memorials of Edward Burne-Jones*, ii. 265.

D

Rutherford, Morris's old friend Philip Webb said, 'Now don't laugh, I am most surely of a melancholy temperament, and I have found for more than thirty years it has been a good corrective to rub shoulders with Morris's hearty love-of-lifedness.'[1] It was this overflowing energy which prompted his multifarious activities many of which he succeeded in carrying on all at once. It was no uncommon thing to find him in his work-room at Hammersmith writing a lecture, composing a poem, making a design and working at a tapestry loom at apparently one and the same time, and in addition throwing out instructions to his secretary and expletives to no one in particular.

Morris swore like a bargee and in spite of his fundamental kindliness he was as irascible as a porcupine. It did not take much to make the quills fret and fly and they were generally winged with good round curses. All the authorities agree that his capacity in the art of expletive was as vigorous as his vocabulary was original and varied. Unfortunately, however, few examples of this gift have been preserved. Wilfrid Blount gives one. He had taken Morris to Shipley Church where there is a fine Norman tower, 'injured with restoration.' Morris's indignation broke out as they walked up the nave and he swore mightily at the offending parsons: 'Beasts! Pigs! Damn their souls!'[2] Generally speaking, he reserved this gift for those who committed the sins of destroying architecture by restorations, disfiguring

[1] *Letters to Three Friends*. W. Hale White, *n*. 79.
[2] *My Diaries*. Blount, i. 229.

landscapes by advertisement hoardings and unsuitable buildings, or cities by smoke, and for many other evils of a commercially minded era. He was not one to suffer fools gladly any more than he suffered profiteers gladly and both had their share of his expletives. But he must have loved swearing for its own sake or applied it as a general exhaust for all manner of ill-humours, for when there was no particular person or thing to curse he swore half-inwardly to himself. This he called with consciousness of the humour of the situation 'talking to nobody in particular.'

His swearing, though vigorous, was apparently good-humoured. In fact, after early recognition of his gift by his friends, there is little doubt that the histrionic side of him once more came into play and he acted or rather over-acted the part. He liked acting, but, like Garrick, he was probably better off the stage than on. Mackail has not failed to note this characteristic.

'It is not without value as an illustration of his curiously compounded personality,' he says, 'that in the moods when he was not dreaming of himself as Tristram or Sigurd, he identified himself very closely with two creations of a quite different mould, Joe Gargery and Mr. Boffin. Both of these amiable characters he more or less consciously copied, if it be not truer to say more or less naturally resembled, and knew that he resembled. The "Morning, morning!" of the latter, and the "Wot larks!" of the former he

adopted as his own favourite methods of salutation.
And one of the phrases that were most constantly on
his lips, which he used indiscriminately to indicate
his disapproval of anything from Parliamentary in-
stitutions to the architecture of St. Paul's Cathedral,
was, as all his friends will remember, the last recorded saying of Mr. F's Aunt, "Bring him forard,
and I'll chuck him out o'winder." '[1]

There were really two William Morrises. There
was the inspired workman, whose motto was 'If I
can,' and there was the man who enjoyed a 'lark.'
Now the inspired workman was something of a
machine despite the antipathies the very word
aroused. He was autocratic and dominant towards
his co-workers and tireless and ruthless of his own
energy and that of others in the pursuit of his aim.
This side of him had no use for anything in life which
did not contribute to the progress of his work, and
it was a large part of him, perhaps not far short of the
whole of him. It explains his remoteness; it explains
his ultimate unapproachableness. 'He is the most
wonderful man I have ever known,' said Wilfrid
Blount, 'unique in this, that he had no thought for
any thing or person, including himself, but only for
the work he had in hand.'[2] The phenomenon is not
unique, geniuses as well as those who are not geniuses are often absorbed in their work to the detriment
of the amenities of life. Blount believed that Morris

---

[1] *Life.* Mackail, i. 220–221.
[2] *My Diaries.* Blount, i. 240.

had a real affection for Burne-Jones and a tenderness for his own daughter Jenny, and he could be 'nice' with her and with his wife, but that generally speaking he was too absorbed in his work to be openly affectionate or actively kind, so that although 'all the world respected and admired him,' it was doubtful if he had many friends. These things may be true, they are probably, having regard to their source, exaggerated. Blount saw life through a magnifying glass. But he is very near to the heart of the mystery when he says, 'The truth is he would not give an hour of his *time* to anyone, he held it to be too valuable.'[1] This passion for work was also noted and feared by all of his friends. Some went so far as to warn him that he was overdoing it. 'It is rust that kills men, not work,' growled Morris.

It would seem difficult to square these preoccupations and austerities with Morris's equally well authenticated *bonhomie*. He was the apostle of a new gospel of fellowship – 'fellowship is life and lack of fellowship is death,' he said through the mouth of John Ball, the hedge-priest of Kent, who is the vehicle of his deepest social ideal. Fellowship was by no means absent from Morris's life. Blount doubted whether he would have had more than half a dozen friends. But which of us has more – or as many? A man with six real friends must have a genius for friendship. Six is enough and Morris may not have had more or so many, but he had battalions of acquaintances, co-workers in his crafts and causes,

[1] *Id.* i. 240.

admirers and miscellaneous hangers-on. His social evenings at Hammersmith, his house-parties at Kelmscott, his constant visits to other people's houses, and above all fellowship with Burne-Jones with its record of Sunday morning visits extending over thirty years, suggest that both friendship and sociability were also among the arts he practised.

Those who knew him best and who knew his passion for work were always surprised at the amount of leisure he could command, and at his readiness to join in any talk or idle fun that was going. His tastes, those which may be called private, were usually sociable. He loved conversation for its own sake, although he himself generally played a boisterous and often stormy part in it. He would argue a point till, and not always metaphorically speaking, the furniture was broken. He was a devotee of the eminently sociable game of bowls, and although a keen angler, he preferred to fish from a punt in the company of a friend or so with whom he could exchange views or badinage when fish were shy. He was even sociable, as we have seen, when composing poetry which he could do and did do in rooms full of talking people; and his reading, the most unsociable of all harmless pleasures, not only took up little time, for he tore the heart from a book with remarkable speed, but the books he read latterly and perhaps always for the sheer fun of the thing were such eminently popular and sociable authors as Dickens, Borrow and Surtees (he revelled in Mr. Jorrocks); he read and quoted with glee *Uncle Remus* and *Huckleberry Finn*, and he loved to go a-riding with William Cobbett and knew *Rural Rides* almost by heart, and it comes as a pleasant surprise to learn that he enjoyed Thomas Love Peacock. These literary recreations were, of course, additional to his life-long love of Chaucer and Froissart, the old Romances, and, of course, Ruskin and Carlyle.

In addition to all this he was a good trencherman. He looked upon cookery as one of the arts and knew a great deal about it in theory and something in practice. He had a *gourmet's* judgment in both food and wine:

And they with rest, and pleasure, and old wine
Began to feel immortal and divine.[1]

One of his favourite illustrations of the decadence of England from its medieval state, his biographer tells us, was the barbarism of modern English cooking and especially the abuse and disuse of vegetables.

'There are two things,' Morris said, 'about which women know absolutely nothing, dress and cookery: their twist isn't that way. They have no sense of colour or grace in drapery, and they never invented a new dish or failed to spoil an old one.'[2]

He was here talking for effect, twisting truth's tail. He enjoyed the surprise and amiable conster-

[1] *The Earthly Paradise*. 1890 Ed., 127.
[2] *Life*. Mackail, i. 224.

nation which followed a paradoxical statement or
a perverted or side-tracked truism. But he was
no epigrammatist or paradox-monger. The very
robustness of his character, his buoyancy and
sailor-like breeziness, were expressed in his talk
more emphatically than elsewhere, and it is clear
that he was sufficiently boisterous and dogmatic
in statement to impress or even to shock others,
without deliberate effort for mere effect. During the
old Queen's Square days he and Watts-Dunton often
lunched at the Cock in Fleet Street, Morris liked the
'sanded floor and quaint old-fashioned settles.' The
day after their first visit, when Watts-Dunton was
lunching there again with another poet, the waiter
who knew him well said: 'That was a loudish gent
a-lunching with you yesterday, sir. I thought once
you was a-coming to blows.' Morris, says Watts-
Dunton, was only declaiming against the Elizabe-
than dramatists, especially Cyril Tourneur.[1]

This boisterousness was no mere pose. It often
resembled a reaction from arrested vitality, a sudden
fear at the thought of boredom, and it was therefore
closely allied with his overweening love of work.
Throughout all his books two themes are constantly
recurring. One is consciousness of the evanescence
of earthly life and the other, fear of boredom. Work
conquers the first in so far as it can be conquered by
handing on the tradition of your skill and you joy in
it, and also by making you forget, and art is a pro-
phylactic for the second. Leisure would be a burden

[1] *Old Familiar Faces.* Theodore Watts-Dunton, 247–248.

without art. This was his religion, and it spread out
to an infinitude of faith in the coming of a better
world for humanity, not hereafter, but here and in
time. He called himself a Pagan, and so probably
he was, in the sense that Marcus Aurelius and Plato
were pagans; but there is little direct evidence of
his inward faith. Both Blount[1] and Bruce Glasier[2]
say that he did not believe in a God, the Creator
of the world; but he was neither a dogmatist nor a
pessimist.

Morris, 'feeling kindly unto all the earth,' grudg-
ing 'every minute as it passes bye,' was a healthily
going concern only when at work; when he stopped
working he was like those students who relieve their
innate boredom between studies by the gentle art of
ragging. His high spirits expressing themselves
boisterously were a sort of rag. Morris liked a lark
– 'Wot larks!' – and he yielded to the need of companionship in himself and others, but when he
stopped work he was faced with boredom, so he filled
in the time by kicking over the traces. This theory
is supported by his own *News from Nowhere*. The

[1] *My Diaries*. Blount, i. 229.
[2] See *William Morris and the Early Days of the Socialist Movement*, chap. xvii. On one occasion, Bruce Glasier records that Morris
once told a Salvationist that he would like his God to be 'a big-
hearted, jolly chap, who'd want to see everybody jolly and happy
like Himself. He would talk to us about His work, about the
seasons and flowers and birds and so forth, and would say "Gather
round, boys, there's plenty of good victuals and good wine also –
come, put your hand to and help yourselves, and we'll have a pipe
and a jolly and a merry time together." ' Pp. 165–166.

people in his delectable Utopia had made work so joyful that their one fear was that there would not be enough of it to go round. William Morris was in the opposite position, he had found so much good and joyous work to do and so few capable of doing it that he had to do most of it himself, and he was constantly haunted by the presence of 'quick-coming death' who strove to close upon him before the great enterprise was accomplished.

All his friends say that Morris was in love with life, that he enjoyed life with a fullness of joy granted to few. Theodore Watts-Dunton saw him always as a 'radiant boy of genius' even when 'the years had silvered his hair and carved wrinkles on his brow, but left his blue-grey eyes as bright as when they first opened on the world.'[1] The evidence supports the statements but only in a special sense. Morris loved life, but if he enjoyed living, and there is no reason to doubt it, it was only to the extent that he was able to live on his own terms. So long as he was beating at the ivory gate of the Morrisian Eldorado all was well. When that was impossible life became empty and dull; he was really happy when he was working full time and full speed. Some one complained to him that a chair he had designed was uncomfortable. 'If you want to be comfortable,' said Morris, 'go to bed!' That anecdote is a full-length portrait of William Morris. And another portrait, full-length as well but from another angle, rises triumphantly out of the concluding words of a conversation he had late in life

[1] *Old Familiar Faces*. Theodore Watts-Dunton, 241.

with Watts-Dunton. 'I have enjoyed my life – few men more so – and death in any case is sure.'[1] Death came swiftly, too, and at the fullness of his powers, as he would have wished; and death came painlessly, as those who loved him and who love his memory would have wished.

[1] *Id.* 242.

CHAPTER SIX

The Idea of Handicraft

*

WILLIAM MORRIS stands out among the great figures
of the Victorian Era not so much because he was a
visionary, there were many such, but because he strove,
not without success, to transmute his dream into the
currency of everyday affairs. If he dreamt and sang
of a world in which heroes once dwelt, the world of
Arthurian and Scandinavian legend, he worked hard
to make the world about him worthy of a new race of
heroes as yet unborn. The Golden Age for William
Morris was not only in the past, it was in the future,
and he believed that the new Golden Age could be
brought ever nearer by the simple process of putting
your joy of life into every job of work which fell to
your hand. He loved beauty, wherever it may be or
whatever it may be, but his love was not yearning, it
was action. The Holy Grail was as real to him as it
was to the Knights of the Round Table, but much
as he loved those knights and their lost causes and
impossible ideals, and magnificently as he re-created
their legends in a quaintly bastard language, half
his and half Malory's, he was no pale knight, wanly
loitering for the favours of some willowy wench such
as his friend Burne-Jones loved to depict entangled
in the barbed briar-roses of unrequited love. Morris
was the reverse of pale and so was his philosophy. He
was a child of the Romantic movement but he was
not romantic, and although he could babble of fairy
lands forlorn with the best of his brother bards, he
believed that the Holy Grail could be sought with

most chance of capture in the workshop where useful and beautiful pieces of goods were made and in
the company of men who were in revolt against the
unseemliness and the waste of modern civilization.
William Morris was unique among eminent Victor-
ians because he strove to practise what he preached.
He was a 'dreamer of dreams,' as he knew, but
he was also striving to 'put the crooked straight.'
The dream was not enough. 'My work,' he said, as
long ago as 1856, 'is the embodiment of dreams in
one form or another.'[1] He challenged the triumphant and invincible ugliness of his surroundings
with the dream of a city beautiful. He had vision to
see what was wrong, and in the name of that vision
he threw down the gage, and ever afterwards carried
on a kind of holy warfare in favour of joyful work and
fine as distinct from bulk production.

He saw the drab chaos of our big towns and the
dull lives led by their vast populations, and he strove
to show how it was possible for men to work happily
together and to make the products of their hands
both seemly and useful. He saw that men took no joy
of their work, and little pleasure in the things they
made. There was little depth or fine quality in life,
and no margin to the page of existence. All experiences were controlled by mercenary standards; it was
asked of all things not whether they were good or
useful or beautiful, but whether they were market-
able. Without this last they were considered to be of
no value. Yet, in the midst of it all, he believed that

---

[1] *Life.* Mackail, i. 107.

men were not dead to all sense of beauty or incapable of appreciating a fuller and deeper life free of the tinsel and glitter of the market-place; he believed that the door had but to be opened for humanity to walk joyously into the Utopia of his dreams.

The war he waged was not a war of destruction. He sought to vanquish a sordid and ugly world by building up a generous and beautiful one. Beautiful things were to be made that would in themselves change the world, that would not only be so beautiful as to give significance to their mean and ugly surroundings, but that would have the effect of making men feel this meanness and desire to undo it. By virtue of a rare imagination, coupled with tireless practical and administrative ability, he proved that in certain circumstances the renaissance of such beauty was a possibility; for whatever may now be thought of his design as such, or his taste as such, whatever differences of opinion there may be among artists and critics with regard to his æsthetics, which were not his but Ruskin's, there cannot be two opinions that his methods pushed to their logical conclusion and universally applied, provided that he had not been born so far out of his due time as to make such a proceeding impossible, would have turned an unseemly hive of acquisitiveness into a social organism of grace and dignity.

William Morris did not claim originality for his ideas, and he was never weary of owning John Ruskin as his master. But it was not so much his genius for expounding ideas as his skill in giving ideas practical form which made him unique among the men of his period. Rarely has human being possessed the ability of expression in so many forms. He will be remembered as the motive force behind a number of activities, each of which gained in power and beauty by association with the magic of his enthusiasm. But although his work took many forms, it was extraordinarily homogeneous, and closely and intimately related with his ideal of a new social order. Without this organic relationship between his art and his ideas, the works which bear the mark of his genius are no more than the objects of any mere fashion that passes away. Whether as weaver or decorator, printer or designer, his work is a constant and deliberate protest against cheapness, and an assertion of the principle of production for use against the prevalent one of production for profit; he demands the substitution of a qualitative for a quantitative standard of production. It is an appeal to society to take up the half-forgotten traditions of the pre-commercial age, to go back for its ideals to an age which was interested in what it made, not because of any monetary profit that might accrue therefrom, but because it desired what it produced for its own use, and took a sane joy in the effort of making things that were to be a part of its daily life.

The avowed aim of Morris as a craftsman was to apply and amplify the principles of art laid down by Ruskin in the chapter of *The Stones of Venice* called 'The Nature of Gothic.' He considered the essay one of the most important of its author's works, and that in future days it would be considered 'one of the very few necessary and inevitable utterances of the century.'[1] Its central principle that art is the expression of man's joy in his work, received the ardent support of Morris; it was his adherence to this principle more than anything else which constituted that discipleship which he so frankly admitted, not, perhaps, without the exaggeration of gratitude for early inspiration natural to a generous temperament. For although in one sense he was a practical Ruskin, he departed from his master along more ways than one. He was derivative mainly in the sense of having been awakened by the teachings of Ruskin to the possibilities of that joyful craftsmanship in which his genius found full expression. There was an affinity between the two men which was, quite naturally, first revealed by the elder. This affinity was almost complete, but it broke down in one essential. Morris, 'born out of his due time,' as he cried, child of the Middle Ages as he undoubtedly was, was yet never so consistent a medievalist as Ruskin. He would go back to the Middle Ages with Ruskin for the lost traditions of craftsmanship, but beyond that his medievalism did not go. Ruskin's love of even the best days of Feudalism did not convince Morris of the desirability of their revival. The traditions of art lay in the past, but the progress of society lay in the future. Ruskin called himself a Tory of the old type;[2] Morris was an avowed Socialist.

[1] Preface to the Kelmscott edition of *The Nature of Gothic*, 1892.
[2] In later life Ruskin confessed to a leaning towards Socialism.

Morris based his theory that art was the expression of man's joy in his work, on his own desire for happiness, which he could not help believing was a universal desire. He argued that his life was under the influence of two dominating moods, which he called the mood of energy and the mood of idleness. These two moods, now one, then the other, were always crying out to be satisfied. The mood of energy could only be satisfied by action, that of idleness by memory of pleasurable experiences, of beautiful things or places. He found also that while the mood of idleness amused him, that of energy gave him hope. And he believed that all men's lives were compounded of these two moods. From this he deduced that the aim of art was to administer to these moods, first by giving men pleasurable means for the expression of their energy, and by thus producing beautiful things giving them worthy objects for joy in idleness. Further, he says:

'I believe that art cannot be the result of external compulsion; the labour which goes to produce it is voluntary, and partly undertaken for the labour itself, partly for the sake of the hope of producing something which, when done, shall give pleasure to the users of it. Or, again, this extra labour, when it *is* extra, is undertaken with the aim of satisfying that mood of energy by employing it to produce something worth doing, and which, therefore, will keep before the worker a lively hope while he is working; and also by giving it work to do in which there is

absolute immediate pleasure. Perhaps it is difficult
to explain to the non-artistic capacity that this definite sensuous pleasure is always pleasant in the handi-
work of the deft workman when he is working suc-
cessfully, and that it increases in proportion to the
freedom and individuality of the work. Also you
must understand that this production of art, and consequent pleasure in work, is not confined to the production of matters which are works of art only, like
pictures, statues, and so forth, but has been and
should be a part of all labour in some form or other:
so only will the claims of the mood of energy be
satisfied.

'Therefore the Aim of Art is to increase the happiness of men, by giving them beauty and interest of
incident to amuse their leisure, and prevent them
wearying even of rest, and by giving them hope and
bodily pleasure in their work; or, shortly, to make
man's work happy and his rest fruitful.'[1]

The essential qualities of art were decoration and
design. The form itself would be beautiful in proportion as its design accorded with Nature. It must
not only look as if it had, as it were, grown under
man's hands, it must look as if it could go on growing; or, rather, that it would neither be obtrusive
amid natural surroundings nor an impediment amid
those devised by the inventiveness and labour of men.

'For, and this,' he says, 'is at the root of the whole
matter, everything made by man's hands has a form,

[1] *Signs of Change*. (1888.) 121–122.

which must be either beautiful or ugly; beautiful if it is in accord with Nature, and helps her; ugly if it is discordant with Nature, and thwarts her.'[1]

Decoration was the final expression of the artist's appreciation of, and happiness in, his work under these conditions, and the expression of his desire to give others pleasure in that work. 'To give people pleasure in the things they must perforce *use*, that is the great office of decoration; to give people pleasure in the things they must perforce *make*, that is the use of it.'[2]

Acceptance of this theory cancels the modern habit of segregating art from the common affairs of life. It turns art from a private into a public, from an exclusive into a popular, thing; and it invites, nay, necessitates, the happy co-operation of the whole community in its production. Art must become, as it was at one time, architectonic, or, in other words, organically related and subservient to the master-craft of architecture, or better still, merged in that co-ordination of all the arts whose final form is the greatest of all masterpieces, a beautiful city. Morris had no sympathy with any art which did not fall under this law. The only genuine art was applied art. Every art product must have some definite relation-ship with private house or public building. Painting was more and more to take its place as an adjunct to architecture; it was to become mural, putting the

---

[1] *The Decorative Arts.* (1878.) 5.
[2] *Hopes and Fears for Art.* (1882.) 4.

final touches to the builder's work in glowing decorations. Sculpture was to be the blossoming, as it were,
of the stonework of homestead, workshop, or meet-
ing-place. These were parts of the decorative expression of the artist's work. Painting and sculpture were
to be kindred to the decoration of a cup or a vase,
a woven fabric or a printed cloth, or a piece of furniture. He carried his love of applied art even into the
realm of music, in which he had little interest except
when it took the form of folk-song or old church
music, where harmony and melody are woven into
activities and devotions of a people.

But if art, as understood by Morris, were to make
the 'fine arts' superfluous, and the maker of refined
luxuries, bric-à-brac, articles of *vertu*, platform music
and easel pictures unnecessary, it would also raise the
workman above the line of drudgery by making him
happy in his work and free of the tyranny of the
machine, which would be relegated to relieving men
of the monotony of tasks which were degrading, dull
or otherwise objectionable. Instead of the artist, as
we now understand him, living a pampered or neg-
lected life according to the measure of his success in
making things which are complete in themselves and
unrelated to the activities of life by which men live,
we shall have the craftsman. He will make things for
use, which shall be so beautiful that any ornaments
apart from them will be unnecessary. But the craftsman will not be an exclusive person like the artist;
he will be the common worker, no longer the slave
of a machine, but one who has joy in the work of his

hands into which he weaves his vision of the world, and by which he expresses and interprets the wonder and mystery of life.

William Morris realized fully the coming tendency towards standardized production, and he saw in this movement the destruction, not of happiness alone, but of the soul of man. The artist had become the dependant of a small cultured class; he ministered to their exclusive tastes, whilst the great body of the people toiled at the duplication of utilities which were often rendered useless and even dangerous by imitation and adulteration. Morris demanded for each individual the right to express his own personality in the things he made. He looked upon mechanical industry as little better than a slave system which destroyed alike the joy of life and the opportunity of generous and dignified social growth. His gospel of work was a demand for the liberation of personal expression as much as for the Ruskinian joy in work; this latter would indeed follow as a natural consequence when men were once more free to exercise brain as well as brawn in the things they made.

'The hope of pleasure in the work itself: how strange that hope must seem to some of my readers – to most of them! Yet I think that to all living things there is a pleasure in the exercise of their energies, and that even beasts rejoice in being lithe and swift and strong. But a man at work, making something which he feels will exist because he is working at it and wills it, is exercising the energies of his mind and soul as well as his body. Memory and imagination help him as he works. Not only his own thoughts, but the thoughts of the men of past ages guide his hands; and, as a part of the human race, he creates. If we work thus we shall be men, and our days will be happy and eventful.'[1]

Throughout his life this view of art dominated him. Its earliest intimations, felt rather than known, came to him when he roamed the hornbeam glades of Epping Forest as a child; later, it filled him with wonder at Marlborough College, when he devoted hours, usually spent in play or study, to the contemplation of the medieval survivals in the architecture of that neighbourhood; and later still, when he found opportunities of visiting Normandy and Flanders, the wonders of craftsmanship in Rouen, in Amiens, and in Bruges deepened still more his consciousness of the need for a renaissance of unity between art and work. His intense love and deep understanding of medieval architecture and craftsmanship can be traced through all his writings, from their beginnings in his contributions to the *Oxford and Cambridge Magazine*, in 1856, down through poem, romance, and essay, to the ardent lectures of his later years – lectures given to art workers in London, Birmingham, Burslem, and elsewhere, to the Society for the Protection of Ancient Buildings, and to innumerable Socialist and Reform organizations all over the country.

[1] *Signs of Change.* (1888.) 144.

The dominant characteristic of all these impressions and utterances is the high value set upon the work produced under the guilds of the Middle Ages. The craft-guilds appealed to Morris because they represented a condition of labour which was both fair to the workman and honest to the consumer, and in addition because that, down to their hour of supremacy in the beginning of the fourteenth century, they were quite democratic in constitution. There were no mere journeymen, and apprentices were sure, as a matter of course, to take their places as masters of the craft in the ordinary course of events. William Morris, however, never actually advocated the restoration of the guild system, but few will doubt that he would have found a more congenial *milieu* for his political efforts among the Guild Socialists of to-day than he found among the Social Democrats of his own time.

The three main arguments advanced by Morris in favour of reversion to the medieval tradition of production, in addition to the insistence laid by the guilds upon soundness of material and deftness of craftsmanship, were:

(1) *Absence of division of labour;* giving the craftsman an interest in the actual and complete article he was making, instead of, as nowadays, in only one part of it, as for instance in, say, the making of tables, where the craftsman of the past would be a maker of actual tables and not, like his descendant, the modern cabinet-maker, a maker of one part of a table. Or, again, in the making of boots, where the division of

labour ordains that in the factory-made boot each part is segregated for a specialized operation, and no 'operative' constructs a complete boot. Under such conditions there can be no real interest in the final form of an article, and no joy in the various and separate operations which go to its construction. The worker is robbed of the joy that follows his conscious-ness of the organic relationship of the results of his labour, and his work deteriorates accordingly in character, and too often, in quality.

(2) *The direct relationship between craftsman and consumer;* the craftsman, being thus enabled to con-sider the personal needs of his customer, and so to weave into his labour the consciousness of the plea-sure of the ultimate user with that of his own pleasure as maker of the article.

(3) *The local nature of craftsmanship;* that is, the production in one district, or one country, of all articles that the resources of the locality make prac-ticable. Thus saving cost of transport, and adding to the personality of the craftsman the distinction of character which only environment can give to goods.

It was, he claimed, these three incidents of crafts-manship which gave in a large measure that beauty, naturalness, and exquisite proportion which marked the objects produced under the guilds of the Middle Ages. Speaking of the breaking up of that system, Morris said:

'What I wish you chiefly to note and remember is this, that the men of the Renaissance lent all their

energies, consciously or unconsciously, to the sever-
ance of art from the daily lives of men, and that they
brought it to pass, if not utterly in their own days, yet
speedily and certainly. I must remind you, though
I, and better men than I, have said it over and over
again, that once every man that made anything made
it a work of art besides a useful piece of goods, whereas
now only a very few things have even the most distant
claim to be considered works of art. I beg you to
consider that most carefully and seriously, and to try
to think what it means. But first, lest any of you
doubt it, let me ask you what forms the great mass of
the objects that fill our museums, setting aside posi-
tive pictures and sculpture? Is it not just the common household goods of past time? True it is that
some people may look upon them simply as curiosities, but you and I have been taught most properly to
look upon them as priceless treasures that can teach
us all sorts of things, and yet, I repeat, they are for the
most part common household goods, wrought by
"common fellows," as people say now, without any
cultivation, men who thought the sun went round the
earth, and that Jerusalem was exactly in the middle
of the world.'[1]

The lesson William Morris would have us learn
from a fragment of domestic crockery handed down
to us from those remote days, when 'common' men
built the great minsters, the noble manor houses, and
the simple, yet dignified cottages and barns of Eng-

[1] *Art and the Beauty of the Earth.* (1881.) 11–12. Ed. 1898.

land, is that the idea which inspired the potter was
the same as that which moved the mason to pile stone
on stone in the building of edifices which are still the
glory and the joy of men. The household utensil, no
less than the great east window of York Minster; the
tapestry in the baronial hall, no less than the many-
coloured walls of St. Mark's at Venice, were but
parts of one great popular art. The aim of Morris
was to restore and to give modern significance to that
art.

A true architectural work was not then the mere
design and masonry of a building as we understand
that word, but a building designed and equipped
both as regards structure and contents in harmony
with its ultimate purpose. Architecture is the art of
civilization; but noble as it is in itself,

'it neither ever has existed nor never can exist alive
and progressive by itself, but must cherish and be
cherished by all the crafts whereby men make the
things which they intend shall be beautiful, and shall
last somewhat beyond the passing day. Further, it is
this union of the arts,' he says, 'mutually helpful and
harmoniously subordinated one to another, which I
have learned to think of as Architecture.'[1]

Architecture, then, was the art which expressed in
a large, embracing manner the value of life and at
the same time augmented that value. Architecture
was useful and necessary as any useful and necessary
work of man; but added to this utility was the power

[1] *Hopes and Fears for Art.* (1882.) 169–170.

of historical record, æsthetic expression, and even
moral inspiration. Every building erected in the true
spirit of architecture was the expression of the aspirations and needs of the race. But to possess this true
spirit it must have been founded on the happy work
of the major part of the population, namely the craftsmen or, as we should say, the workers. 'Architectural beauty,' he said, ' is the result of the harmoni-
ous and intelligent co-operation of the whole body
of people engaged in producing the work of the
workman.'[1] Work as he did towards a rehabilitation
of this spirit, Morris was under no illusion as to the
practicability of its revival under present commercial
conditions. What he advocated, what he worked for,
was a renaissance of the spirit which underlay Gothic
art as he understood it, and that, in his own words,
could only come about in its completeness, 'as a part
of a change as wide and deep as that which destroyed
Feudalism.'[2]

[1] *Gothic Architecture.* (1889.) Kelmscott edition, 1893, 56.
[2] *Id.* 65.

CHAPTER SEVEN

The Revival of Handicraft

*

IT is significant, but perhaps not surprising to learn, that his first practical efforts in the direction of reviving homogeneous art were forced upon him by his inability to purchase any domestic furniture of modern manufacture worthy, in his opinion, to be placed within the walls of the Red House which he had built for himself at Upton. Characteristically the needs of that house were to be the genesis of a revolution, still proceeding, not only in furniture and design, but in the conditions of labour under which these things were made. The idea of craftsmanship actually came to him at an earlier date, for some time prior to the building of the Red House, Morris had come to be as dissatisfied with art or craft divorced from architecture, as he came to be dissatisfied with the division of labour. He had started to paint pictures under the influence of Rossetti and the Pre-Raphaelites, but it was not long before he had convinced himself that pictures could have no legitimate status apart from design, and he came to believe that to have devoted his time to painting of this kind would have been as idle a thing as if he were to have devoted his life entirely to writing poetry.

It was with such ideas and tastes that he approached the problem of house-building when that problem came within the ambit of his own needs. The need for a house was something more than the establishing of a home, it was an opportunity for giving actual form to previously established tastes and convictions. Morris was aware of the difficulties in the way of furnishing a house on this plan. He and Burne-Jones had had a foretaste of them when furnishing their rooms, in Red Lion Square. But he was a 'dreamer of dreams,' who was not content with the mere vision. No vision, howsoever beautiful in itself, satisfied William Morris. He was never happy unless he was turning his dreams into realities. He was a romantic but no sentimentalist; the end of his romance was always practical power with a creative objective.

That movement, which came to be known as the Arts and Crafts Movement, first became conscious of itself during the building of the Red House. The mere architecture had been easy, for in the architect, Philip Webb, Morris had found a kindred spirit. Furnishing the house along the prescribed lines of quality and beauty in design, craft and materials was the real problem and the outcome was the founding of the first workshops of modern times to be controlled by artists. This took the form of the establishment of the workshops at Merton Abbey and the shop in London, still known as Morris and Co. This move was not actually initiated by Morris. It arose out of the conversations of his circle, the painter, Ford Madox Brown, being probably the first to suggest the actual idea of an establishment for the sale of products made under the new conditions. But it was soon realized that the energy and initiative of the enterprise came from Morris who, as we have seen, eventually became the sole proprietor of the concern. The revival of handicraft attracted many young artists, and in a few years there were craftsmen working in various parts of London and the provinces, and these afterwards organized or joined handicraft guilds and societies for the promotion of their work. William Morris, however, was not an original promoter of any of these organizations, although he was one of the first members (and afterwards a master) of the Art Workers' Guild, founded in 1884, and of the Arts and Crafts Exhibition Society, founded in 1888, into both of which he threw his energies and enthusiasms along with such men as Walter Crane, T. J. Cobden-Sanderson, Emery Walker, Professor W. R. Lethaby, Heywood Sumner, and his old friend William de Morgan.

The unique contribution of William Morris to the handicraft movement was an ideal craftsmanship, a point of view and a policy in one. The simple fact that he was a man of many parts and tireless energy practising what he preached was sufficient to co-ordinate an impulsion towards qualitative as distinct from quantitative production which was already a conscious characteristic of the new spirit. The need for good design being recognized, he did not content himself with the mere advocacy of good design, he made himself a good designer; and in the same way he taught himself craft after craft. In some instances he had not only to revive an almost lost art, he had to learn how to make the materials of the art, because none could be found that were free from the blight of degeneration. A good instance may be observed in connection with his revival of the handicraft of weaving. When the process reached the stage of dyeing he found it impossible to procure reliable vegetable dyes, and as he would not use the then novel synthetic dyes which were coming into use, he went down to Leek in Staffordshire, and worked at the vats until he produced what he wanted. His power of application and concentration made him one of the most unique and varied craftsmen of all time. For, of the numerous crafts connected with the business of Morris and Company, there was not one of which he did not understand the theory and, in most instances, the practice as well. It was in this versatility that he departed conspicuously from the methods of the Middle Ages where master-craftsmanship was a form of specialization. The varied genius of William Morris recalls Leonardo da Vinci and Michael Angelo: he would without doubt have been equally at home in the fifteenth, as in say the twelfth century.

The rich colourings of his fabrics, with their beautiful and strong designs; his tapestries, stained glass, wall-papers, chintzes, no less than the noble books of the Kelmscott Press, have all been epoch-making in their own ways. And although Morris dwelt so much in the past and sought so much to link up modern craftsmanship with that of the Middle Ages, his work is in no sense imitative. He was never a copyist. His design and the quality of his products followed the medieval tradition only in spirit. They are a continuation, a development of

the handicrafts of that period but characteristic of
the present day, as though being true to nature
they possessed capacity for growth and power of
adaptation to changing needs. In a lecture delivered
before the Trades' Guild of Learning, in 1877,
he said, speaking of ancient art, 'Let therefore us
study it wisely, be taught by it, kindled by it; all the
while determining not to imitate or repeat it; to have
either no art at all, or an art which we have made our
own.'[1] Morris not only gave but followed that advice.
He went to the Middle Ages, to the Craft Masters of
the great guilds for instruction, and for inspiration,
but he learnt from them how to make an art of his
own, just as they had made an art for themselves.

The modern craftsman differed from the craftsman of the past in one outstanding particular. He
was more conscious of his art. His work has not that
simplicity, that *naïveté* which characterizes so much
of the work of the ages which had not ceased to
wonder at the world. This was inevitable in the
deliberate reformer. But although Morris did what
he did with full consciousness of the object and
meaning of his work, his consciousness was too great
ever to become a pose or a mannerism. He saw the
social relationship between art and life so clearly that
had such a vision been possible to the Middle Ages,
capitalism might never have been born, and Morris
would not have had to plead with his age in strong
and beautiful English words for the re-acceptance of
art in daily life:

[1] *The Decorative Arts.* (1878.) 18.

'The world has in these days to choose whether she will have art or leave it, and that we also, each one of us, have to make up our minds which camp we will or can join, those that honestly accept art or those that honestly reject it. . . . If you accept it, it must be part of your daily lives, and the daily life of every man. It will be with us wherever we go, in the ancient city full of traditions of past time, in the newly-cleared farm in America or the colonies, where no man has dwelt for traditions to gather round him; in the quiet country-side as in the busy town, no place shall be without it. You will have it with you in your sorrow as in your joy, in your workaday hours as in your leisure. It shall be no respecter of persons, but be shared by gentle and simple, learned and unlearned, and be as a language that all can understand. It will not hinder any work that is necessary to the life of man at the best, but it will destroy all degrading toil, all enervating luxury, all foppish frivolity. It will be the deadly foe of ignorance, dishonesty, and tyranny, and will foster goodwill, fair dealing, and confidence between man and man. It will teach you to respect the highest intellect with a manly reverence, but not to despise any man who does not pretend to be what he is not; and that which will be the instrument that it shall work with and the food that shall nourish it shall be man's pleasure in his daily labour, the kindest and the best gift that the world has ever had.'[1]

[1] *Art and the Beauty of the Earth.* (1881.) 16–17. Ed. 1898.

CHAPTER EIGHT

The Kelmscott Press

*

THERE are never any difficulties in the way of understanding the aims of William Morris as a craftsman, because, being engaged in a mission of reforming zeal as well as in the inspired game of artistic creation, he was careful to explain, step by step, what were the specific objects of his craftsmanship. This is particularly true of his last and in many ways most spectacular and probably most permanent, craftwork. The Kelmscott Press was no fad. It was not a rich man's hobby. It was not a commercial adventure. William Morris was a printer with a purpose none the less, but the purpose at that time was rare, for it was to be a good printer, as he had been a good weaver, a good dyer, a good designer, a good writer and a good citizen. His object in founding the Kelmscott Press is stated with admirable clarity.

'I began printing books,' he wrote, 'with the hope of producing some which would have a definite claim to beauty, while at the same time they should be easy to read and should not dazzle the eye, or trouble the intellect of the reader by eccentricity of form in the letters.'[1]

Those few words contain the whole of his faith as

[1] *A Note by William Morris on his Aims in Founding the Kelmscott Press.* (1898.) 1. (This was the last book printed on the Kelmscott Press. The *Note* has been re-printed in an Appendix to Halliday Sparling's *The Kelmscott Press and William Morris.* 1924.)

a printer, and they possess within them the explanation of the weakness as well as the strength of the noble typographical work of his ripest years. Weakness, in that his innate love of decoration inclined him, not always, but often to think of the page in terms of ornament instead of in terms of type, and strength, in that he applied to the making of books those fundamental ideas of excellence in design and quality which had been the dominating principles of his life-work and which were now full of experience and ripe with long achievement in many crafts.

The Kelmscott Press was the outcome of much thought upon printing and the making of dignified books covering something like a quarter of a century. An examination of any of the books written and published by Morris, even the pamphlets and leaflets issued for propaganda purposes, reveals a conscious effort towards a better typography than was then current. S. C. Cockerell tells us that as early as the year 1866 an edition of *The Earthly Paradise* was projected, 'which was to have been a folio in double columns, profusely illustrated by Sir Edward Burne-Jones, and typographically superior to the books of that time.'[1] Thirty-five of the blocks were cut and specimen pages set up in Caslon type at the Chiswick Press, but the project was abandoned. During these years also Morris had practised the art of manuscript with his usual distinction, and collected and studied

[1] 'A Short History and Description of the Kelmscott Press.' (1898.) Included in Sparling's volume containing Morris's *Note*.

examples of the finely printed books of the early presses. But no more practical steps were taken towards a deliberate and consistent attempt to revive good printing until towards the close of the eighteen-eighties when his interest in typography was fired and co-ordinated by the enthusiasm and practical experience of his friend and neighbour at Hammersmith, Emery Walker, whose views on printing coincided with his own. These ideas were set forth in a paper contributed by Emery Walker to the Catalogue of the Exhibition of the Arts and Crafts Exhibition Society, held at the New Gallery, in 1888. Morris was fully in accord with the ideas: they had, in fact, been formulated in consultation with him, and the immediate result was a closer contact with printing which ultimately developed into the establishment of the Kelmscott Press.

The first step towards that end was an attempt to produce books according to the Emery Walker formula through one of the best of the commercial printing offices. The first experiment was made at the Chiswick Press with Morris's own romance *The House of the Wolfings* with results so promising that Morris was encouraged to repeat the experiment, adding to the next attempt the result of the experience with the first. In the following year (1889) what amounts to a typographical victory was won with *The Roots of the Mountains*, which so gratified the author-typographer that he declared it to be 'the best-looking book issued since the seventeenth century.' This was perhaps an exaggerated verdict born of the enthusiasm of the moment;[1] at the same time the book marks an epoch in the revival of good printing, few examples of typography have had such a widespread influence, and it still remains an admirable piece of typography, showing at once the best application of Caslon's old face type, and the correct proportions of a printed page. The book is dignified and practical, fulfilling the common sense of book production, that is by being pleasing and appropriate in form and easy to read, and to that extent a better example of good printing than many of the more personal and grandiose masterpieces of the Kelmscott Press.

It would be wrong however to assume that Morris's adventure into the realm of printing was merely a matter of typographical reform. As usual in all that concerns design Morris was both a benevolent revolutionary and a beneficent reactionary. He went back to go forward and his reaction was to discover the point in architectonics where design, quality and purpose were most admirably related. His aim was therefore not so much to revive good printing as to revive good book production. He was not primarily interested in typography, but all his life he had loved a beautiful book. He had collected manuscripts and incunabula; he had tried his hand,

---

[1] This enthusiasm was very real. 'I am so pleased with my book,' Morris said, soon after it was published, ' – typography, binding, and must I say it, literary matter – that I am any day to be seen huggling it up, and am become a spectacle to Gods and men because of it.' *Life*. Mackail, ii. 227.

with distinction as usual, at writing and illuminating
the former and now aimed at reviving the latter, for
Morris as a maker of books at the Kelmscott Press
did no more than re-create the conditions under
which the incunabulæ were produced, and the
Kelmscott books remain examples of incunabulæ not
so much born out of their due time as born again and
born different. His influence on good printing began
and ended with *The Roots of the Mountains* and the
theories which inspired that production. Those
theories were applied to the work of the Kelmscott
Press, but they included in this later and more
personal application extensions into the realm of
decoration which have no inevitable relationship
with good printing. This departure from the straight
and narrow path of typographical rectitude is
explicable only in terms of the Morrisian idiosyncrasy for decoration as the climax of design. He was
naturally efflorescent; he liked to exfoliate. As a
designer and a craftsman he knew what good printing
was, but as a man and a lover of rich ornamentation he
so obviously shrank from the austerity of the frankly
utilitarian page that one is almost forced to the conclusion that at this stage of the revival of good
printing there were two distinct influences with two
equally distinct results and tendencies. The first
might be called the revival of *good printing*, that is to
say printing which should have no other object than
to serve as the shortest line of communication
between author and reader; and the second might be
called the revival of *fine printing*, or printing which

aims at combining the primary objects of typography with the secondary objects of decoration and luxurious format. It may be fairly and safely assumed that the influence of Emery Walker, which was the deciding factor in bringing Morris into printing, is all towards a revival of *good printing*, in which of course he had Morris's full support, as their combined work on *The Roots of the Mountains* proves, and the logical conclusion of such an influence would not be the decorated volumes of the Kelmscott Press but the formal typography of the Doves Press. William Morris, on the other hand, whilst still and always respecting and encouraging that printing which can be both excellent and fit for 'human nature's daily food,' yearned for *fine printing* in all its splendour, bursting into harmonies of flower and leaf on the most opulent of hand-made paper, and panoplied in vellum or richly tooled leather. The climax of the one was the Doves *Bible*, and of the other, the Kelmscott *Chaucer*, and if both reach their apex in those bibliographical realms where only millionaires can breathe, the situation is not so ironical as at first it might appear to be, for the inaccessible splendour of the fine printing which Morris inaugurated became the aspiration of all typographers, and although the idea of Morris was often degraded by the base coinage of commercially minded imitations, it laid the foundations of that general movement which has made good printing to-day accessible to anyone who wants it.

The desire for good printing was beginning to be felt in many directions. But the directions were far removed from the presses which supplied reading matter to the general public. They were generally the result of the enthusiasm of amateurs who either liked well-printed books for their own sake or thought that by setting an example of good printing all book production would tend to improve in quality. In the first class was Dr. C. H. O. Daniel, Provost of Worcester College, who printed many charming books on his press at Oxford, and in the second, in addition to William Morris and Emery Walker, there were Herbert P. Horne and Selwyn Image, who had shown taste and skill in the production of *The Hobby Horse* (1886–92), and Charles Ricketts and W. L. Hacon who, with the publication of *The Dial* (1889), took the first step towards the foundations of the Vale Press which ultimately came under the influence of Morris and produced many notable books.[1] Good book production was thus in the air when Morris turned his imagination and skill in craftsmanship to the subject. 'What I wanted,' he said in his *Note* on his aims in founding the Kelmscott Press, 'was letter pure in form; severe, without needless excrescences; solid, without the thickening and thinning of the line which is the essential fault of the ordinary modern type, and which makes it difficult to read; and not compressed laterally, as all type has

[1] For a fuller account of this movement see *The Eighteen Nineties*, by Holbrook Jackson, 'The Revival of Printing,' chap. xix, pp. 255–266.

grown to be owing to commercial exigencies. There was only one source from which to take examples of this perfected Roman type, to wit, the works of the great Venetian printers of the fifteenth century, of whom Nicholas Jenson produced the completest and most Roman characters from 1470 to 1476.

'This Type I studied with much care, getting it photographed to a big scale, and drawing it over many times before I began designing my own letter; so that though I think I mastered the essence of it, I did not copy it servilely; in fact, my Roman type, especially in the lower case, tends rather more to the Gothic than does Jenson's.' This was called the Golden type. It was Roman in character with, as Morris admitted, certain evidences of his Gothic predilections; these were so pronounced that it was not long before he felt he must have a Gothic as well as a Roman fount, and thus he came to design the Troy type, so named after the first book for which he used it, *The Recuyell of the Historyes of Troye* (1892). In this fount he 'strove to redeem the Gothic character from the charge of unreadableness which is commonly brought against it.' Later on he was forced to design another type to meet the necessities of the Kelmscott *Chaucer*, a folio in double column, which he called after the book. Equal care was taken with regard to the rest of the materials which go to the making of the perfect book; paper was specially made by hand, vellum for binding was specially procured from Rome, other coverings and the ribbons for ties were specially made, and Morris designed and had specially cut his own initial letters and decorations, whilst Burne-Jones and other artists designed his illustrations in harmony with the typography. Care also was taken with the ink, and Morris at one time thought of making his own ink, but this intention was never carried out. During 1890 he was experimenting with his types and other materials, and on the 31st of January in the following year the first trial sheet was printed on the Kelmscott Press, which had been set up in a cottage close to Kelmscott House on the Upper Mall, Hammersmith.

The first book to be printed on the new press was Morris's own romance, *The Story of the Glittering Plain*. The press-work was completed in April of that year, and *Poems by the Way*, again his own work, was set up and printed. There was consistency in this preferential treatment of his own compositions, a consistency in key with the logical procedure of his progress from decorative artist to complete craftsman. It was not that he set his own works higher than those of others, but that a poem or a story by William Morris was not complete until it had been set forth in the best materials and workmanship which he could command.[1] But the same treatment of the works of others quickly followed; the books printed however make no claim to being representative of any kind of literature or any particular

[1] Morris printed nineteen of his own original works or translations on the Kelmscott Press.

period; they represent in the main the literary prefer-
ences of the printer and in most instances they are
frankly acts of homage to his favourite authors.
Before, in fact, the Kelmscott books begin to be of
public interest as inaugurators of a revival in printing,
or even treasures for the bibliophile, they must be
looked upon as the contents of such a library as
William Morris would have included in his personal
dream of Utopia.

Book after book now came from the press in more
or less regular succession, Morris's enthusiasm and
interest growing with every production. The method
was slow and deliberate, there was nothing of the
hustle which is so characteristic of a modern printing
office, and yet the output was almost as notable in
quantity as in quality. The Kelmscott Press existed
as a going concern for a little over seven years from
the printing of the first sheet in January, 1891, to
the completion of the final volume by his executors
in March, 1898. During that time fifty-two works,
in sixty-six volumes, were printed and published, and
in addition eighteen lists of the books printed or
in preparation; twenty-nine announcements relat-
ing to individual books; nine various items such
as programmes, invitation cards and leaflets, etc.;
and two trial pages of the projected but never
realized edition of Berner's *Froissart*. Great variety
was also achieved, for although a Kelmscott book
is unmistakable in its individuality, each separate
work has its own special characteristics, pleasing
and expressive variations in characters and initials,

decorations and pictures, composition, lay-out and size.[1]

The sizes range from the friendly 16mo's, such as Rossetti's *Hand and Soul*, *The Friendship of Amis and Amile*, and Morris's lecture on *Gothic Architecture*, and the equally companionable 8vo's, like Tennyson's *Maud* and his own *News from Nowhere*; through small 4to's: Ruskin's *Nature of Gothic*, and Morris's *Dream of John Ball* to the large 4to's such as Caxton's *Historyes of Troye*, the second issue of *The Story of the Glittering Plain*, and *The Well at the World's End*, until the final consummation of the press is reached in the great folio *Chaucer* which must always remain one of the world's greatest examples of typography.

The history of the *Chaucer* is specially interesting as that work not only engaged so much of William Morris's interest during his final years, but it may be taken as an epitome of the press as well as its triumphant consummation. In 1891 Morris was already dreaming of a Kelmscott *Chaucer* printed from a specially designed type, and as early as January, 1892, one year after the foundation of the press, he was printing trial pages of *Chaucer* in the Troye type, which proved too large. He then decided to have that character re-cut in the size

---

[1] One of the works, *The Story of the Glittering Plain*, was printed twice in small 4to in 1891, and in large 4to in 1894. The total number of copies of all books printed at the Kelmscott Press was 18,234, representing a turnover of £50,000. *The Kelmscott Press and William Morris*. H. Halliday Sparling. 72.

known as pica, and this he called the 'Chaucer' type. Trial pages were made and approved in July of that year and the idea of the *Chaucer* as we now know it was definitely established. Wilfrid Scawen Blount was at Kelmscott Manor early in the month, and records that he found 'Morris in fine spirits, and inexhaustible energy over his new hobby, the printing press. He is beginning a *Chaucer*, and there is great discussion whether it is to be in single or double column.'[1] In April it had been announced as in preparation, and further announcements, containing additional information and amendments, appeared from time to time.

The first sheet was printed in August, 1894, and that month a notice to the trade said that there would be 325 copies containing about sixty-three woodcuts by Burne-Jones. Three months later it was decided to increase the number of illustrations to upwards of seventy and to increase the number of copies by 100. The list for December, 1894, announces that all copies are sold. A specimen page was shown at the Arts and Crafts Exhibition in 1893. From 1894 the work of composing and printing was proceeding and an extra press was started in 1895; from that time both presses were exclusively used for the *Chaucer*. The last page of *The Romaunt of the Rose* was printed on 10 September. On 8 May, 1896, a year and nine months after the printing of the first sheet, the book was completed. The first two copies were in the hand of Morris and Burne-Jones on 2 June. Four hundred

[1] *My Diaries*. Wilfrid Scawen Blount. i. 67.

and twenty-five copies were issued on paper at twenty pounds, 13 on vellum at 120 guineas, bound in half holland; 48 copies, including two on vellum, were bound at the Doves Bindery in full pigskin from a special design by Morris.

It is no exaggeration to say that the happiness of the final months of his life was largely dependent upon the progress of this book. Mackail records Morris's quaint distress when there was a temporary hitch in the printing, and how in the end he came to live for the day upon which the *Chaucer* would be complete and in his hands. As its completion came nearer, Morris became nervous about anything which threatened, however remotely, to delay it. 'I'd like it finished to-morrow,' he answered, when asked how early a date would satisfy him for its appearance: 'every day beyond to-morrow that it isn't done is one too many.'[1] Later, in his own library, on what was to be his last Christmas Eve, a visitor looking over the sheets that were lying on the table remarked on the greater beauty of those pages following the *Canterbury Tales* where picture-pages face one another. Morris was alarmed.

'Now don't you go saying that to Burne-Jones,' he said, 'or he'll be wanting to do the first part over again; and the worst of that would be, that he'd want to do all the rest over again, because the other would be so much better, and then we should never get

<hr>

[1] *Life.* Mackail, ii. 322.

done, but always be going round and round in a circle.'[1]

Burne-Jones, however, was not disturbed, and the last of the eighty-seven pictures was finished two days after Christmas, 1895.

Burne-Jones was as anxious as Morris about the great book. He was in at the earliest discussions of the project in 1891.

'The friends sat down dutifully to read *Chaucer* over again before beginning their work,' writes Lady Burne-Jones, 'and infinitely funny it was when Morris occasionally professed to be taken prosaic and not to understand what the poet meant. Edward had his own heart-searchings: "I wonder, if Chaucer were alive now, or is aware of what is going on, whether he'd be satisfied with my pictures to his book or whether he'd prefer impressionist ones. I don't trust him. And if he and Morris were to meet in heaven, I wonder if they'd quarrel." '[2]

And again, towards the end, in a moment of discouragement with his drawings, he says:

'I want to show Morris the new *Chaucer* designs: he tells the truth always, and I shall know if he likes them. If he likes them they are very good – but I doubt . . . To-day I feel disappointed as I look at them, but I shall know when he has seen them.

[1] *Id.*, ii. 322.
[2] *Memorials of Edward Burne-Jones*, ii. 217.

Inexorable judges, both of us – no appeal when we condemn.'[1]

But their fears were groundless as they knew on that memorable June day when the first copies were placed in their hands.

The *Chaucer* is the keystone of the Kelmscott Press, it completes and supports the arch of its achievement. In its rich pages, in its opulent size, its typographical and bookish majesty, are all that Morris knew or dreamt of in the making of a beautiful book. Time cannot do other than increase its beauty. It will mellow like one of the great cathedrals which he loved and, indeed, resembles them in other ways. The Kelmscott *Chaucer* is a cathedral among books, a monument of the best decorated periods of Gothic.

Its sister books of the press are also monumental. It was Morris's dream that such books might be exemplars for all books. He thought them practical and fit for everyday use, if not now, in some Utopian future. The dream was characteristic, for he was a man of action, a craftsman rather than a student. His reading was done early and he came to look upon books as works of art, shrines of noble thoughts and imaginings and desires, and it was more in homage to great writing than out of any wish for its dissemination that he created the Kelmscott books. 'Books that can be held in the hand, and carried to the fireside, are,' said Dr. Johnson, 'best of all.' No one would take a Kelmscott book to the fire, not even

[1] *Memorials of Edward Burne-Jones*, ii. 260.

before it had become so rare as to require a glass case. Those who love books will desire to have at least one Kelmscott, to satisfy the same instinct for homage which prompted Morris's printing. For the rest these books must remain monuments to great authorship and inspirations towards fine printing, and ultimately also as they have been to a greater extent than any other modern books, encouragements to all printers towards good craftsmanship.

CHAPTER NINE

Revolt Against Civilization

*

THE life of William Morris is a complete example of orderly progress from idea to practice, from feeling to action, from the simple to the complex, and it is of special interest because the sequences developed naturally and logically, apparently from their own volition, much as inferences may be drawn from established precedents. In the jargon of modern psychology, his response to certain stimuli could always be postulated. Once this progress pitted itself against the ugliness and inferiority of the merchandise of the times, it was inevitable that it would find itself opposed sooner or later to the conditions under which the goods were made; which is precisely what happened.

William Morris had a natural preference for beautiful objects. He was not content to drug himself against ugliness with poetry and pictures. The beautiful and useful objects he desired could not be purchased in the shops so they must be made specially for him. But the art of making them was almost lost so that it was only with great difficulty that they could be procured, if at all, therefore he must set to work and make them for himself and for others of like tastes. This brought him into conflict with the quantitative system of production with its necessary haste, vulgarity, standardization and monotony and, most pernicious of all, its financial valuation of results. From this point it was only a step into the political arena, and as Socialism was the

only political doctrine which provided any hope at
that time for the logically minded believer in qualitative production, it was inevitable that Morris
should have become a Socialist.

But there were other reasons. Morris not only
loved beautiful 'pieces of goods' as he called them,
but he dreamed of a free and beautiful civilization in
which men might create beautiful things by the work
of their hands in joyful fellowship. He believed that
some such condition existed in the best period of the
Feudal system and that Socialism might reconstruct
something of the best of that lost, for him, Golden
Age. Morris was always true to himself and his
evolution was a genuine unrolling of personality.
His sense of fellowship was evident in his early years,
it prompted that early unfulfilled dream of a monastic life, and the plaintive note of his earlier poems,
even down to *The Earthly Paradise*, is not confined,
as so much of the poetry of the Pre-Raphaelites is, to
vague regret over the evanescence of earthly joys and
the hopelessness of mortal desires. His poetic com-
plaint is against the ugliness and the pain in the life
he saw around him, but unlike most poets, the song
for him was not a thing in itself, he sought as always
the materialization of his dreams, and even in those
of his songs which are not frankly propagandist the
note of revolt is often sounded, although sometimes
it is little more than the stock plaint of the poet
against things as they are. But Morris was in
earnest, and if he complained, he sought redress as
well.

If there is such a thing as Socialist temperament,
Morris possessed it. He thought socially and acted
socially instinctively, and his acceptance of the
principles of Socialism was as inevitable as his
adoption of the craftsman's career. His Utopia was
a craftsman's paradise, a land flowing with William
Morrises. This is not inconsistent with occasional
loss of faith, or desire to abandon a fight in which the
odds against him were so great. Such temporary
reactions befall the upholders of all causes, and to
argue from them that Morris was never in full
sympathy with Socialism, or that he had made an
error which he eventually corrected, is to miss the
real lesson of his life. No proper understanding of
his many-sided career can be obtained without full
recognition of his Socialist phase, for, as Professor
Mackail points out:

'His innate Socialism – if the word may for once
be used in its natural sense and not as expressive of
any doctrine – was, and had been from his earliest
beginnings, the quality which, more than any other,
penetrated and dominated all he did.'[1]

It cannot be too often repeated that, for William
Morris, politics, no less than art, had no meaning
unless they had some direct bearing upon life. His
ideas upon politics, just as his ideas upon art, were
first given a humanistic turn by Ruskin. 'It was
through him,' he says, 'that I learned to give form to
my discontent, which I must say was not by any

[1] *Life.* Mackail, i. 338.

means vague.'[1] Apart from the desire to produce
beautiful things the controlling passion of his life
was a determined hatred of modern civilization, in
which he saw nothing but 'a decaying system, with
no outlook but ever-increasing entanglement and
blindness.'[2]

In his early manhood he had been a passive
holder of the Liberal political faith, or perhaps,
to be more exact, a follower of the Radical section of the Liberal party, for with Liberalism of
the *laissez faire* school, he ever had the most profound contempt. He voted with his party, when
he did vote at all, and even on rare occasions
attended public meetings. But his hatred of all that
is vague both in politics and art was soon to sever his
connection with obscurantist party politics. Towards
the end of the eighteen-seventies his lectures on art
and life express his growing discontent with modern
social conditions, and in 1878, during the opposition
to Lord Beaconsfield's Eastern Policy, his loss of
political faith is seen in a letter in which he alludes to
'the cowardice of the so-called Liberal party.'

His first step in public affairs was taken in 1877,
when he founded the Society for the Protection of
Ancient Buildings; and at about the same time he
aided, with money and work, the Eastern Questions
Association, which was formed to fight the Government on the political crisis of the moment. He threw
himself heart and soul into the organization, and

[1] *How I became a Socialist.* (1896.) 11.
[2] *Signs of Change.* (1888.) 115.

throughout the Russo-Turkish War, was its treasurer. In the May of that year the Association issued an address 'To the working men of England,' written by Morris, in which his attitude towards those who were engaged in an attempt to plunge the country into an entirely mercenary war, indicates a movement of his political ideas towards the revolt against a commercial civilization. He alludes to the bitterness in the hearts of a certain section of the richer classes, and to their hatred of progress. He speaks of the way this hatred is veiled in the newspapers, 'in a kind of decent language,' and with what insolence they refer to the working man: 'These men cannot speak of your order, of its aims, of its leaders, without a sneer or an insult; these men, if they had the power (may England perish rather!), would thwart your just aspirations, would silence you, would deliver you bound hand and foot for ever to irresponsible capital.'[1]

These words are in the traditional manner of the advocate of Socialism, and the man who wrote them could not have been far removed from that faith; but as yet, like many men of his day, and like some still in our own day, he had not realized that Liberalism and Socialism were fundamentally opposed political doctrines and that one could never lead by easy constitutional stages into the other. So for a little longer he remained a Liberal. The first signs of his break with Liberalism came in the following year, during the controversy on the same Eastern Question. He

[1] *Life*. Mackail, i. 349.

wanted to organize a great demonstration against the war-party at Agricultural Hall, and succeeded in getting Gladstone's promise to speak. He booked the hall and got all ready, when 'our Parliamentaries began to quake.' Even the Eastern Questions Association took fright. The meeting fell through, although, Morris wrote, 'Gladstone was quite ready to come up to the scratch, and has behaved well throughout.' The Parliamentary caution of this affair was too much for Morris. The art of compromise was not among his gifts, and it is not surprising to learn that he was chagrined by his first adventure in public life, from which he speedily retired to the more congenial atmosphere of his own workshop.

Two years passed, however, before he finally broke with Liberalism. In 1879 he was treasurer of the National Liberal League, an association formed by those working-class representatives who had become politically conscious of their needs during the agitation against the Eastern Policy of the Government. The Liberals came into power at the General Election of 1880 on a wave of popular feeling against Lord Beaconsfield's policy. Morris's faith, held to his old party now only by the slenderest thread, gave way entirely during the next year. The Irish Coercion Bill of 1881, and the gradual fading away of all promised social reforms in the mists of class privileges and interests and party tactics combined to bring about the final rupture. The National Liberal League was dissolved, and Morris

turned from the old political parties for ever. He
became an avowed Socialist, and joined the Democratic Federation (afterwards the Social Democratic
Federation, and later the Social Democratic Party)
in January, 1882.

Such are broadly the events which marked the
final passing of William Morris into political
Socialism. But eloquent as they are as further in-
dications of his restless desire to get something done
in a political and social crisis which he considered
critical, they bear only a superficial relation to the
inner life of the man and his practical mission. He
was always a temperamental Socialist, and it only
required a certain conjunction of circumstances to
make him feel that some political expression was
required of him. The events just narrated were
among the more obvious of the determining circumstances at this period of transition. At the same time
he had wrestled with the intellectual basis of
Socialism. His mind had been profoundly moved
by the theories of Fourier and Robert Owen, and he
had come into contact with Socialist leaders like
H. M. Hyndman, whom he first met in 1879,
Belfort Bax, and H. H. Champion. In addition it
must not be overlooked that there was a decided
Socialist tendency of the kind that might have been
derived from the humanitarianism of Ruskin, among
the craftsmen and art-workers of the time, similar,
as a matter of fact, to that underlying desire for
better conditions for workmanship which was at the
root of Morris's own unrest. The decorative artists

were thus caught up by the economic ideas which were beginning to form the intellectual and emotional currency of many years of scattered and incoherent discontent.

It was through art really that Morris became a Socialist, and he would not have remained of that political faith for five minutes if he had not believed that Socialism could give him conditions under which he could produce the art he desired and which he thought others ought to desire. When he joined the Democratic Federation he was 'blankly ignorant of economics.' He had never so much as opened Adam Smith and scarcely heard of Ricardo or Karl Marx. He had, however, read some articles of John Stuart Mill in one of the reviews, in which the economist attacked Fourierist Socialism. 'In those papers,' says Morris, 'he put the arguments as far as they go, clearly and honestly, and the result so far as I was concerned, was to convince me that Socialism was a necessary change, and that it was possible to bring it about in our own day.'[1] But his own account of his 'conversion' through art, and his growing discontent with the civilization that made the production of the things he liked best impossible, may be accepted as nearer the real truth. Speaking of modern civilization, he wrote:

'What shall I say concerning its mastery of, and its waste of mechanical power, its commonwealth so poor, its enemies of the commonwealth so rich,

[1] *How I became a Socialist.* (1896.) 10.

its stupendous organization – for the misery of
life? Its contempt of simple pleasures which every
one could enjoy but for its folly? Its eyeless vulgarity which has destroyed art, the one certain
solace of labour? All this I felt then as now, but I did
not know why it was so. The hope of the past times
was gone, the struggles of mankind for many ages
had produced nothing but this sordid, aimless, ugly
confusion; the immediate future seemed to me likely
to intensify all the present evils by sweeping away
the last survivals of the days before the dull squalor of
civilization had settled down on the world. This was
a bad look-out indeed, and, if I may mention myself
as a personality and not as a mere type, especially so
to a man of my disposition, careless of metaphysics
and religion, as well as of scientific analysis, but with
a deep love of the earth and the life on it, and a
passion for the history of the past of mankind.
Think of it! Was it all to end in a counting-house on
the top of a cinder heap, with Podsnap's drawing-
room in the offing, and a Whig committee dealing
out champagne to the rich and margarine to the poor
in such convenient proportions as would make all
men contented together, though the pleasure of the
eyes was gone from the world, and the place of
Homer was to be taken by Huxley? Yet, believe me,
in my heart when I really forced myself to look
towards the future, that is what I saw in it, and as
far as I could tell scarce anyone seemed to think it
worth while to struggle against such a consummation
of civilization. So there I was in for a fine pessimistic

end of life, if it had not somehow dawned on me, that amidst all this filth of civilization the seeds of a great change, what we others call Social Revolution, were beginning to germinate. The whole face of things was changed to me by that discovery, and all I had to do then in order to become a Socialist was to hook myself on to the practical movement, which, as before said, I have tried to do as well as I could.

'To sum up then, the study of history and the love and practice of art forced me into a hatred of the civilization, which if things were to stop as they are would turn history into inconsequent nonsense, and make art a collection of the curiosities of the past, which would have no serious relation to the life of the present.'[1]

These words, written towards the end of his life, represent the real attitude of Morris towards Socialism. When he declared himself a militant Socialist by joining the Democratic Federation, in 1883, the impulsion towards Socialism, which had received its first serious set-back with the failure of the Paris Commune some twelve years earlier, was just beginning to pull itself together again. In England, as on the Continent, its rebirth had come about in an acute burst of political consciousness. The organization, founded by Henry M. Hyndman in 1881, was its first organized expression in this country. It was the outcome of an attempt, more or less opportunist, to co-ordinate the Chartism of

[1] *How I became a Socialist.* (1896.) 11–12.

the 'forties and 'fifties with the youthful Radical-
Socialism then awakening among the working
classes. In principle, the Social Democratic Federation was Marxian; and its aim was to organize the
proletariat with the distinct object of capturing the
land and capital, and administering these for the
benefit of the commonwealth. Its propaganda took
the form of education towards political representa-
tion on uncompromising Socialist lines.

CHAPTER TEN

Militancy and Disenchantment

*

WILLIAM MORRIS threw himself into the fray with that whole-hearted enthusiasm and superb energy which characterized all his work. He joined the executive of the Federation, lectured at open-air meetings and indoors, both in London and the Provinces, wrote for *Justice*, which was established shortly afterwards out of funds provided by Edward Carpenter and, later on, kept going with money provided by himself, and did in general any work, no matter how hum-drum, that he found ready to his hand.

In these early days, the very youth of the Socialist movement, apart from the rawness and inexperience of most of its members, made dissensions inevitable. And Morris had barely been a member of the Social Democratic Federation for two years when a split came, and he and his followers left Hyndman and formed the Socialist League. The actual rupture came about at a conference on 28 December, 1884, and the League was formed in the following January. Tempers ran high and hard words were used on both sides. But some years afterwards Morris owned that he had been in the wrong. 'Many years ago,' he said, just before his death, at a meeting in support of Hyndman's candidature, at Burnley, 'Hyndman and I had a great quarrel. Now I want you fellows to understand that he was quite right and I was quite wrong.'

Socialist propaganda and action was in its experimental stage, and the various possibilities of the

movement were as yet either in the raw state of
'unattached' Socialism, or else creating frictions
within the one and only organization that existed.
And the chances of bringing the various ideas to
some sort of independent expression upon their own
lines were considerably impeded by the fact that up
to then Socialism and Anarchism in England had not
been properly defined. The upholders of each set of
ideas were indeed rowing in the same boat, with such
confusion as may be imagined. The first body to
extricate itself from this tangle was the Fabian
Society, formed in 1883 to carry on a non-sectarian,
educational, and constitutional propaganda, with
'permeation' as its watchword. This society captured the least aggressive and most of the abler
middle-class Socialists. The Socialist League drew
away from the Social Democratic Federation the
idealists and the anarchists, and left the older
organization free to carry on its work for independent Socialist action.

The actual cause of Morris's difference with the
Federation was mainly political. His idea then was
that the time was not ripe for independent parliamentary action. But this was only the most obvious
feature of his discontent. His one distinct aim,
apart from the decided political (in the Platonic
sense) bent of his craftsmanship, was to make
Socialists. His motto was 'Education towards
Revolution,' and he wished to do this as usual without compromise, free on the one hand of the necessary intrigue and compromise of parliamentary

action, and on the other of the limitations of doctrinaire teachings. The Socialist League was the
inevitable outcome of the vitality of the moment. It
was the natural abiding-place of those Socialists who,
like Morris, fell between the two stools of the
doctrinaire, 'straight-ticket' Socialism of the Social
Democratic Federation and the administrative compromise of the Fabians. The League had a short
career and a somewhat tragic end.

Morris became a more ardent propagandist than
ever when the Socialist League started. He was its
chief initiator, guide, and financier. In 1885 he
started and ran *The Commonweal*, first as a monthly,
and then as a weekly, contributing to its pages
articles and poems and two of his finest prose
romances, *A Dream of John Ball*, and *News from
Nowhere*. But with all his fine enthusiasm and
tremendous zeal he could not interest the British
public in his organization. In the following year,
however, what Morris failed to do by good work
was done by accident. There had been an attempt
on the part of the police to prevent public gatherings
at the corner of Dod Street and Burdett Road. The
spot had long been recognized as one of London's
street forums, and the Social Democratic Federation
and the Socialist League determined to assert the
right of Free Speech by resisting the police. This
they did, somewhat mildly, but not so mildly as to
prevent the police arresting eight of the demon-
strators. The next day one of them was sentenced to
two months hard labour. There was a scene in court

and cries of 'Shame!' Morris, who was in court with
other Socialists, took part in the expression of feeling,
and in the attempt to restore order there was some
hustling, when he was arrested for disorderly conduct
and striking a policeman. He gave a direct negative
to this charge, and was released. The whole affair
was slight enough in its way, but it was an attempt
to defend the right of Free Speech, and the advertisement the League got out of the incident sent it
with a bound into something like popularity.

In the same year there were other similar dis-
turbances, in one of which Morris was arrested for
addressing an open-air meeting off the Edgware
Road. Two days afterwards he was convicted at
Marylebone Police Court for the technical offence of
obstruction and fined a shilling and costs. More
serious events than these took place during that and
the following year. The unemployed meeting in
Trafalgar Square on 8 February, 1886, which ended
in the mob breaking the windows of West End
clubs, stopping carriages and demanding money
from the occupants, and breaking into and looting
several shops, filled the authorities with something
like panic. Indeed, many people thought that the
events of those winter months were the beginning of
an insurrection. The police, at any rate, arguing that
prevention was better than cure, determined to
suppress as many open-air meetings as possible, and
to keep a strict watch upon all street processions.
These tactics culminated in Trafalgar Square on
13 November, 1887.

A meeting of protest against the Irish policy of the Government had been announced to take place in the Square, and forbidden by the police. A political gathering of an inoccuous type was thus turned into a demonstration in favour of Free Speech, in which all the Socialist, Radical, and advanced societies of London took part. There was an immense crowd and, besides a small army of constables, two squadrons of Life Guards were requisitioned. In addition the Square was occupied by a battalion of Foot Guards, with fixed bayonets and twenty rounds of ammunition. There was no untoward event until an effort was made to clear the Square, when amid the scuffling which followed a young man named Alfred Linnell was killed. Morris did not reach the Square until nearly all was over. He had marched with a Socialist column of six thousand strong from Clerkenwell Green, which had been charged and dispersed by the police in Shaftesbury Avenue.

All these events contributed to the brief popularity of the League. But Morris was gradually losing confidence in it. In the first years of his militant Socialism he saw revolt blazing on the near horizon, and fully believed that a short and effective struggle would bring Socialism in his own time; but experience ultimately convinced him of the error of such a hope. It would take time both to change the heart and develop the administrative genius of men. But he was under no illusion as to the value of social palliatives, and whilst looking upon the growth of

H

Labourist Socialism with its decided bureaucratic
tendencies as inevitable, he knew that, in spite of all
the remedial social measures of well-intentioned
reformers, without Socialists there could be no
Socialism. 'Make Socialists,' he said, in his parting
words to the League. 'We Socialists can do nothing
else that is useful.' In his heart he knew that he had
attended the obsequies of an ideal.

He left the Socialist League in 1890, the year
following that in which the executive had been
captured by the Anarchist Group who had deposed
him from the editorship of *The Commonweal*. All
that was effective in the League was now centred in
the Hammersmith Branch, which met in an annexe
of Kelmscott House, which Morris had turned into
a lecture hall. The rest had drifted into the ranks of
the Fabian Society and other reform organizations.
This branch remained faithful to him, and on his
secession from the League it became an independent
Socialist Society. The League itself went from bad
to worse. It became the platform of incapable and
ineffective revolutionaries until it expired in 1892,
when Nicoll, the editor of *The Commonweal*, was
sentenced to eighteen months' imprisonment for an
incendiary article following the conviction of the
Walsall Anarchists. His break with the League left
Morris a more or less passive Socialist. He still had
faith in the idea of Socialism, but that faith was a
reversion to his original and never-abandoned belief
in salvation by craftsmanship.

CHAPTER ELEVEN

A Craftsman's Paradise

*

To understand the position of William Morris as a Socialist, it is necessary to realize exactly what he meant by a term which even now, after so many years of experience and propaganda, has no very exact meaning for the majority of people. This, no doubt, is to a considerable extent inevitable, because Socialism is a theory, and from its very nature can never be an exact science. But there is no reason why the idea behind the theory should not be so defined as to be made quite clear to the average intelligence. The great difficulty in the way of such a clear definition is the fact that the very idea of Socialism involves an extension of individual freedom, spiritual as well as material, beyond any recognized practice in the modern world or any historical precedent, at the same time setting limits to certain freedoms which have been accepted as normal for centuries. Socialism in its broadest sense seeks to make men free by releasing capital, and all that word means, land, labour, machines of production and distribution, from the dominance of private ownership, and investing it in the will of the whole people to be administered for the public good.

All Socialists will agree so far; differences arise when an attempt is made to apply this idea to actual affairs. In this process of differentiation Morris himself took a conspicuous and determined part. In his day, although so very near to our own, the propaganda of Socialism was complicated by the fact that, in the minds of revolutionists even, the divisional line between it and that other social idea, Anarchism, had not been clearly recognized. And further, the difficulties were increased by the absence of any fixed ideas upon the part to be played by insurrection and material revolt in the advocacy of the new cause. Nowadays the first of these difficulties has been removed. Anarchism is admitted to be different from, and even antagonistic to, Socialism. Morris realized this, and, as we have seen, it was the capture of the Socialist League by the Anarchists which finally made him withdraw from militant Socialist propaganda.

The problem of militancy has undergone many changes, but in the last few years it has more or less settled itself, and at the moment there are two clearly defined methods of Socialist procedure in this country. That of the Labour Party which is frankly constitutional and parliamentarian and would only resort even to the strike as an instrument of force in a last extremity; and that of the Communist Party, which is as frankly catastrophic and would organize the workers for the capture of the means of government by force, the seizure of the workshops, banks and other organizations of Capitalism, and the substitution of their owners and governors by a dictatorship of the proletariat. At the time of Morris's death Socialism in England had outgrown its continental teachers, and it had accepted more or less the constitutional usages of the English people; but since the War and the Russian Revolution foreign influences have more than regained their lost ground. The Communist Party is allied with the international movement which has its head-quarters at Moscow. It definitely accepts the methods adopted by the adherents of Lenin and Trotzky in the Revolution of October, 1917, together with the doctrines of Karl Marx.

Morris, with that fine fervour which coloured his whole life, began his Socialist career as a convinced insurrectionist, and in his early enthusiasm he believed it possible to bring about a complete revolution in a few years. But he reckoned without his man power. He found the workers unfitted by character and tradition for such a rapid change; and in the end he became a firm advocate of propaganda by education, and if he still looked to force as a last measure, he realized that catastrophic methods would be negatived unless faith in Socialism together with integrity of purpose had been developed in the majority of the workers. That is what he meant when he advised the League to make Socialists.

But in the days of Morris these were not the only obstacles in the way of a clear view of the Socialist idea. The elimination of the illimitable freedoms of the Anarchists and of the possibly premature catastrophies of the insurrectionists, still left many points to be made smoother. These after a while became confined, in a great measure, to questions of propaganda, the main differences in temperament and circumstance being satisfied in one or the other of the

three Socialist organizations which were the outcome
of the controversies and propaganda of the eighteen-
eighties: the Social Democratic Federation, the
Fabian Society, and the Independent Labour Party.
It was Morris's separation from the first of these and
the consequent formation of the now defunct
Socialist League, that finally differentiated the
Anarchist from the Socialist in England.

But throughout the history of the Socialist movement the process of defining the underlying idea of
Socialism itself has never ceased. After the Anarchist
question had been settled, all sorts of points as to the
limitations of personal freedom in reference to
property necessarily arose, and out of these that
which most affected Morris was the place and quality
of production under Socialism. As was natural with
one whose Socialism was the outcome of a desire to
see the qualities that moved the artist applied to
production, he looked upon any tendency towards
State Socialism and its inevitable dependence upon
the standardization of production, with profound
suspicion and distaste. At the same time he was not
so indifferent to the difficulties in the way of trans-
ferring property from private to collective ownership,
as not to recognize that an uncertain period of State
Socialism stood between Capitalism and the inauguration of a complete Socialist State.[1]

---

[1] This theory of William Morris was discovered to be true in
Russia. The attempt to re-organize that country on a complete
Communist basis after the Bolshevik Revolution, was found to be
impractical, and Lenin was forced to sanction a limited measure of

Such a period was one of the necessary evils of a change for the better. But Morris never tired of endeavouring to make it quite clear (and he went nearer towards accomplishing this than any other writer on the subject) that State Socialism was a means and not an end. Complete Socialism was Communism, and this could never be brought about by mere legal enactment, superimposed parliamentary regulations, or sudden bursts of indifferently informed humanitarian fervour. Socialism could only be realized by something like a revolution in the spirit of the workers which should back up all desire of change with intelligence, courage, and power.

'Intelligence enough to conceive, courage enough to will, power enough to compel. If our ideas of a new Society are anything more than a dream, these three qualities must animate the due effective majority of the working people; and then, I say, the thing will be done.'[1]

The difference between the Socialism of Morris and that of the more recent type of constitutional and political Socialist, the type of Socialist created by the Fabian Society, will now be more clearly recognized. Morris, like the Fabian, had full faith in education towards Socialism, but unlike the Fabian he had

collectivist control or State Capitalism, and even a certain measure of strictly controlled private ownership, pending the complete communalization of the state.

[1] *Communism*. By William Morris. (Fabian Tract, No. 113, p. 8.)

small faith in Socialism by legal enactment. To him the impetus towards the new society must come from within, and when that became intelligent enough, powerful enough, and courageous enough, it would gain its ends. Parliamentary measures without this, be they never so well-intentioned, would be, at their very best, nothing more than palliatives or experiments. And Morris's use of the word 'compel' indicates that he had not finally ignored the possible use of some sort of force. But, in the manifesto of the Hammersmith Socialist Society, which he compiled in 1890, whilst deprecating 'spasmodic and desperate acts of violence,' on humanitarian and tactical grounds, as tending towards increasing the miseries of the poor and the difficulties of Socialists by alarming the timid, he still sees 'that it may be necessary to incur the penalties attaching to *passive* resistance, which is the true weapon of the weak and the unarmed,' and likely to embarrass a tyranny far more than violence could do.

In none of his activities was Morris more 'out of his due time' than in his Socialism. His whole association with the Socialist movement was a tragedy: a tragedy born of the contest between one who was by nature a Socialist, and others who were but the advocates of Socialism. He was so much of a Socialist himself that he could have stepped out of the turmoil of our acquisitive age into the commonwealth of man without the slightest inconvenience. Training and transition were not necessary for him, he was born for the communal life. He had the gifts of disinterested service and joyful work without which Socialism were impossible. That is why he at first imagined his dream could be realized suddenly. Socialism was an extension of himself, a multiplication of William Morris. He did not realize his own rarity until his life was nearly over.

Morris's 'due time' was either in the thirteenth century, or in that future in which his own Utopia lies still unborn. And although he made a mistake as regards the time in which the great revolution could be accomplished, he never for a moment made any mistake about the kind of Socialism he wanted. He was never really a believer in State Socialism, or what we should now call Collectivism, with the whole machinery of production and distribution under the control of an all-powerful central organization, and he would have loathed both the theories and practices of Russian Communism. He demanded complete equality of condition, so that each individual should have sufficient margin to his life for the free play of whatsoever personality and idiosyncrasy he had within him, in so far as their expression in nowise endangered a similar freedom for all. This was what he meant by equality. That prodigal love of colour and design which animated all he ever did was revolted at the regularity and uniformity of such State Socialism as that imagined by Bellamy, or that implied by the institutional methods of either a Sidney Webb or a Lenin, and if he could have imagined no alternative to those ideas he would not have called himself a Socialist at all.

But he visualized an alternative, which was peculiar to himself. The Socialism he advocated and, in so far as he was able, lived, has but a remote connection with the Socialism of others. The Socialism of William Morris was Socialism for William Morris and his like. *News from Nowhere*, with its vision of a pastoral life of humanized association, was Morris's reply to *Looking Backward* with its vast mechanical organization of town life. Association and decentralization were the passwords to his Utopia, and these were to be the means of the fullest expression of that 'pleasure in work itself,' which was the underlying principle of his belief in politics, economics, and art. He was convinced that the problem of the organization of life could not be dealt with by centralization on a national scale, 'working by a kind of magic for which no one feels himself responsible.' On the contrary, he saw that it would be necessary for the unit of administration to be so small as to enable every individual in the community to feel that he was a responsible and interested party in the conduct of the state. His aim was not merely the socialization of property, but the communalization of social feeling, the awakening of social consciousness in such a way as to abolish any sense of the state as a thing apart from the individual.

Communism, Morris thought, would realize itself in the family idea as distinct from the army idea of Collectivism. Instead of the organized regularity of battalions expressed in uniformity, we should have the equality of free groups with a margin for variation. No family would be richer than its neighbour and none would be poor, and the fullest possible freedom would exist for all. So long as there was any necessity for a central State Department its duty would be confined to seeing that no individual allowed the expression of his freedom to interfere with the freedom of another, and to advising upon errors in the production and distribution of the communal property; but as soon as the principles underlying the state were recognized by every one always and intuitively, the last vestiges of centralization would die out.[1] Variety of life Morris considered as much a part of Communism as equality of condition, and this could only be fully attained through work which had become art.

This idea of local administration, based upon the freedom of individuals from economic need and the tyranny of private interests, would spread from the individual to the group or guild, and from thence to the wider field of the whole community, until it finally embraced the civilized world.

'Men will at last come to see,' he says, 'that the only way to avoid the tyranny and waste of bureaucracy is by the Federation of Independent Communities: their federation being for definite purposes; for fostering the organization of labour, by ascertaining the real demand for commodities, and so avoiding waste; for organizing the distribution of goods, the migration of persons – in short, the

[1] *Signs of Change*. (1888.) 201.

friendly inter-communication of people whose
interests are common, although the circumstances of
their natural surroundings made necessary differences of life and manners between them.'[1]

The state would be a federation of individuals,
just as the world would be a federation of communities, and exchange would be friendly instead of
commercial. Rivalry for profit would be replaced by
rivalry of excellence; production would be thus
improved in quality, and the freeing of men from
fashionable or enforced idleness would increase its
quantity also. The waste of cheapness would cease,
and as the anxiety of men became removed entirely
from the economic arena, they would be free to test
to the full the intellectual and imaginative treasures
of life.

[1] *Signs of Change.* (1888.) 200.

CHAPTER TWELVE

The Fellowship of Man

*

THROUGHOUT the work of William Morris there is a robust note of good fellowship not confined merely to man, a 'feeling kindly unto all the earth,' which is constantly finding expression in his own joy in the beauty of the world and his desire to devise means to make that beauty triumphant and its enjoyment common to all. It is no mere pious feeling, still less a piece of sentimentalism; it is a religious conviction, a part of the inner life of Morris, and, like all genuine religious emotion, it has a fighting element, a bugle call, in its composition. This was seen in his militant attitude towards the degradation of human life by commercialism. But it did not end there; he was not only prepared to fight against Capitalism; he would have been equally ready to defend his Utopia if it had been realized. Even in his own day, when he forgot the poverty of the peasants, he saw in the beautiful downs of southern England 'a country-side worth fighting for,' and the White Horse carved on the hill-side by the valorous men of the past, was a sign for him of the valour and courage which might come again. His heroes were dauntless warriors, vikings, and the strong kindly men of his imaginative tales, and his innate democratic sense was not outraged at the idea of service under some intrepid large-hearted hero. 'The only decent official that England ever had,' he said, 'was Alfred the Great.'

His consciousness was Utopian. He lived a double

life, one amidst the turmoil and chaos of a society
which antagonized him at every point, and the other
his real life, in a wondrous realm of happy fellowship
and bright colour, a peaceful sanctuary full of the
activities of useful work joyfully performed and
steeped in a large and reflective leisure. As an artist
his contributions to life were contributions to such
a life as that: materializations of his dream. His
gorgeous tapestries and chintzes; his richly painted
manuscripts and noble books with their pages bursting into flower and leaf; his stained glass, his em-
broideries, his carpets with their beautiful intricate
designs and rich colourings; his dreamful tapestried
romances with their long melodious names – *The
Roots of the Mountains, The Story of the Glittering
Plain, The Waters of the Wondrous Isles, The Sundering Flood, The Wood Beyond the World,* and *The
Well at the World's End,* were not the products of our
age. They were born out of their due time if ever
works of man were. Many of those works of his
stood alone like dream-products amid the modern
waste of vulgar luxuriousness and poor shoddy, for
William Morris was a magician with the power of
turning the stuff of dreams into realities.

His imagination was a panorama of a beautiful
world unborn. Every detail of his vision was exact
and vivid; he actually saw with his mind's eye the
Utopia he wanted. He would have compromised
for some move in its direction, to be sure, but he
never wavered from his own faith, his dream was
inviolable, and he saw at the end of all the chaos and

the reforms, his own bright commune 'in England's green and sunny land.' Towards the end of his life he gave the world, in *News from Nowhere*, a peep into that realm, and through his magic casement amazed eyes look out upon an England grown young again; a happy land of pleasant toil and careless ease. There were no monstrous cities with sky-scraping buildings any more than there were towering personalities or organizations. The familiar backwash of humanity, as we know it in the ugliness of poverty, was as absent as the pestiferous scrap-heaps of our big cities. All was clean and dignified. Men and women went about their work with a deeper joy than we go about our feverish spells of play; and the happiness of their days was expressed in the sincere beauty of their bright and clean little towns. The puckered brow and anxious eyes of the commercial age were replaced by a joyful serenity for work for profit was replaced by work for use. 'The reward of labour is *life*,' they said, and were content, and the one little rift in their happy lute was the fear that work might become extinct.

The communistic gospel of William Morris does not, however, end in a sweet vision of a pastoral Utopia; that is, for the time being, and perhaps for all time, Nowhere. But here in this grim and laborious Somewhere is work to be done. In the vision of this work his gospel grows prophetic, and out of the deeps of his love of men he raises aloft his voice in the cause of fellowship. The religion of Morris is contained in that word. 'Fellowship is life,

lack of fellowship is death,' says the Seer of Kent in
A Dream of John Ball, the book into which Morris
put his fullest utterances upon human life. And,
as if moved by the depth and earnestness of his
theme, this simple story of the peasant rising in
medieval England, represents the highest point he
ever reached as a writer of prose, and perhaps the
highest point of all his work as a writer; for never
before did his pen weave such beautifully worded
and balanced sentences out of his teeming brain. He
became a prophet in telling the tale of a prophet,
he was inspired by the fervour of John Ball, which
corresponded so much with the passion of his own
life. This small book is a parable of fellowship, and
as authentic a gospel, and as necessary to the proper
conduct of life as any book which has ever received
the sanction of religion. *The Dream of John Ball*
is the religion behind the richly coloured dream of
William Morris.

'Yea, forsooth, once again I saw as of old,' says
John Ball to the men of Kent, 'the great treading
down the little, and the strong beating down the
weak, and cruel men fearing not, and kind men
daring not, and wise men caring not; and the saints
in heaven forbearing and yet bidding me not to for-
bear; forsooth, I knew once more that he who
dwelleth well in fellowship, and because of fellowship, shall not fail though he seem to fail to-day, but
in days hereafter shall he and his work yet be alive,
and men be holpen by them to strive again and yet

again; and yet indeed that was little, since, forsooth, to strive was my pleasure and my life.'[1]

Thus strove and taught Morris. He wore the mantle of John Ball, and saw with a full certainty that in fellowship and in emulation alone can life be properly used. He knew for certain that it was not only in the cold 'betterment' of human conditions that the new life would come about, but that in addition to this men would have to realize the essential fellowship of their lives and come to live together as comrades – free of slaves and of masters.

'And how shall it be when these are gone? What else shall ye lack when ye lack masters? Ye shall not lack for the fields ye have tilled, nor the houses ye have built, nor the cloth ye have woven; all these shall be yours, and whatso ye will of what the earth beareth; then shall no man mow the deep grass for another, while his own kine lack cow-meat; and he that soweth shall reap, and the reaper shall eat in fellowship the harvest that in fellowship he hath won; and he that buildeth a house shall dwell in it with those that he biddeth of his free will; and the tithe barn shall garner the wheat for all men to eat of when the seasons are untoward, and the rain-drift hideth the sheaves of August; and all shall be without money and without price. Faithfully and merrily then shall men keep the holy days of the Church in peace of body and joy of heart. And man shall help man, and the saints in heaven shall be glad, because

[1] *A Dream of John Ball.* (1888.) 33.

men no more fear each other; and the churl shall be
ashamed, and shall hide his churlishness till it be
gone, and he be no more a churl; and fellowship
shall be established in heaven and on the earth.'[1]

[1] *A Dream of John Ball.* (1888.) 40.

CHAPTER THIRTEEN
The Man of Letters
★

WHATEVER youthful idea William Morris may have had about the career of letters there is no doubt that he looked upon such a career with little favour as he grew older. This does not mean that he despised literature; such a conclusion is dispelled both by the amount of time he devoted to writing, for Morris set a high value on time, and by his work as a printer and publisher of *belles lettres*: the Kelmscott Press is William Morris's praise of books, his homage to great writing. But he was incapable of looking upon writing, even writing of genius, as an adequate whole-time occupation for a healthy man. With him literature was if not entirely, at least in the nature of a by-product. Long after he had achieved fame as a poet he thought of himself and described himself as a decorative artist. And even in those early days of enthusiasm at Oxford when his undergraduate friends hailed him as 'a big poet' he did not accept the implied bays with the alacrity characteristic of a class of artists which has ever been hungry for praise. On the contrary, he discouraged his admirers by protesting that it was unnecessary to make a fuss about stuff it was so easy to write. He never even referred to himself as a writer of stories in spite of the fact that so much of both his poetry and prose took the form of romantic tales.

He was not, then, a typical man of letters or, indeed, a man of letters in the professional sense at all; he happened to have a knack of writing which produced literature, and very often great literature. It would seem that he could write anywhere and with remarkable ease. An instance is recorded by Walter Crane when he and Morris, travelling from Glasgow, saw from the train the manor house of Yanworth, which he had often heard Morris praise. Shortly afterwards Morris became abstracted and taking paper from the 'wonderful satchel' which he carried in those days, wrote 'furiously all the way back' and produced the ballad called 'The Hall in the Wood,' forty-two verses of four lines each.[1] He never used a study as such; his study, or library, always tended to become a workshop where all sorts of jobs were going on. But this facility is something of an illusion, one with other details of what is already becoming a William Morris legend. His legendary facility was little more than the final act of a long mental process: the writing down of something which he had already composed. If he was capable of writing on his head it was because he had already completed the work in his head. Poetry was thus taken in a daily stride, which happened to be a giant-stride covering many activities. On one occasion it had been noted that he was doing a good deal of muttering to himself whilst working at a tapestry, and that he presently jumped up and rapidly pencilled down a matchless lyric. Upon surprise being expressed that so perfect a poem could be the result of what looked like spontaneous creation, Morris pricked the romantic bubble by saying that he had

[1] Walter Crane. *An Artist's Reminiscences.* 1907. 328.

been telling the lines over to himself for months and had at last got them perfect. This explanation also explains the 'go on talking I am only writing poetry' anecdote, and others of its kind. All of which really explain nothing. They are little more than a round-about way of admitting that William Morris was that rare thing a born writer. Such laconics, with others of their kind, may also be taken as expressions of his hatred of snobbery, particularly of literary snobbery. The fact remains that he had to teach himself all of the crafts which he eventually mastered, except writing, that faculty, like reading, would seem to have come to him naturally. It was probably because of this that he preferred to call himself a decorative artist rather than a poet or a story-teller.

The versatility which he has shown in the decorative arts was equally evident in his work as a literary artist. Here as elsewhere the many facets of his mind reflected the restlessness which so distinguished his genius from that of others and enabled him to reverse the old adage that a Jack-of-all-trades is master of none. Morris mastered every art he practised with a facility which would have been dangerous, if at all possible, with anyone less gifted. It was not that he lacked the laboriousness which even genius may require but that he possessed an audacity of accomplishment which was certainly unique in his generation, and would have been extraordinary at any time. He possessed in a high degree that 'large and flowing personality' regarded by Walt Whitman as the sign of the great man, and this quality is perhaps more obvious in his writings than in any of his works. His friend and brother bard, Swinburne, thought it a defect, and remarked upon it à propos of 'The Lovers of Gudrun,' in a characteristic flash of critical insight.

'I have just received Topsy's book,'[1] he writes to Rossetti in December, 1869: 'the Gudrun story is excellently told, I can see, and of keen interest: but I find generally no change in the *trailing* style of work. His Muse is like Homer's Trojan women; she drags her robes as she walks. I really think any Muse (when she is neither resting nor flying) ought to tighten her girdle, tuck up her skirts, and step out. It is better than Tennyson's short-winded and artificial concision – but there is such a thing as swift and spontaneous style. Top's is spontaneous and slow; and, especially, my ear hungers for more force and variety of sound in the verse. It looks as if he purposely avoided all strenuous emotion or strength of music in thought and word; and so, when set by other work as good his work seems hardly done in thorough earnest. The verses of the months are exquisite – November, I think, especially.'[2]

Morris worked in thorough earnest at everything

[1] *The Earthly Paradise.* William Morris. (Published in parts, 1868–1870.) 'Topsy' and 'Top' were the names by which Morris was known among his friends.
[2] *Letters of Algernon Charles Swinburne, with some Personal Recollections.* Thomas Hake and Arthur Compton-Rickett. 25.

he did, and his writing was no exception, but there is
little doubt that his poetry, and his prose as well,
suffered more than his other works not so much from
his perilous facility as from his prodigious fertility,
aided and abetted by a predilection for the discursive
and the expository. He was long-winded by choice
but he could also be exquisitely concise; for proof
we need only turn to the numerous short stories
in *The Earthly Paradise*, or to the concise and per-
fectly chiselled lyrics in the *Defence of Guenevere*
volume (1858) and to many others sparkling like
jewels among his longer poems. Lyric poetry has
nothing more beautiful of its kind than the four-
versed duet in 'Ogier the Dane,'[1] beginning:

> *In the white-flowered hawthorn brake,*
> *Love, be merry for my sake;*
> *Twine the blossoms in my hair,*
> *Kiss me where I am most fair —*
> *Kiss me, love! for who knoweth*
> *What thing cometh after death?*

And of equal beauty the better-known Nymph's
Song to Hylas from *Jason*, which also appears in
Poems by the Way as 'A Garden by the Sea':

> *I know a little garden-close*
> *Set thick with lily and red rose,*
> *Where I would wander if I might,*
> *From dewy dawn to dewy night,*
> *And have one with me wandering.*

[1] *The Earthly Paradise.* (1890 Ed.) 184.

And though within it no birds sing,
And though no pillared house is there,
And though the apple boughs are bare
Of fruit and blossom, would to God,
Her feet upon the green grass trod,
And I beheld them as before.

And the lesser-known Song from 'The Story of
Acontius and Cydippe' in *The Earthly Paradise*:

Fair is the night and fair the day,
Now April is forgot of May,
Now into June May falls away;
Fair day, fair night, O give me back
The tide that all fair things did lack
Except my love, except my sweet!

Blow back, O Wind! thou art not kind,
Though thou art sweet; thou hast no mind
Her hair about my sweet to wind;
O flowery sward, though thou art bright,
I praise thee not for thy delight,
Thou hast not kissed her silver feet.

It is no reflection upon his high achievement as a
writer to suggest that he is eminently a poet for
selective treatment, and this becomes more evident
when it is recalled that he worked both in lyric and
epic verse, in metrical tale, dramatic episode, and
didactic song, as well as in prose romances, descrip-
tive essays and dissertations upon art and sociology,

and finally in translations from the Greek, the Latin, Old French, and the Norse.

He was primarily a singer and a storyteller. His very facility was bardic, most of his poems, especially the longer ones, suggesting the extemporaneous. In those Middle Ages, out of which, as Mackail says, 'he sometimes seems to have strayed by some accident into the nineteenth century,'[1] he might have been a wandering minstrel if he had not chosen to be a Guild Master. His archaisms are local colour acquired by some unexplained law of spiritual affinity; they are not pedantry, and it is significant, perhaps, that they become less obvious with familiarity. When he read his poems aloud he pitched them to a half-chant, which is also in character, and read thus they have an additional charm. Attempts have been made to trace the origins of his inspiration. Among the ancients Chaucer, Froissart, Malory and the *Sagas* are obviously indicated, and as obviously but less deeply, Browning and Rossetti, among the moderns. But such digging into the archæological strata of poetic genius, interesting though it may be as an exercise in research, is of very little use towards the understanding of a great poet who must stand or fall by the authenticity of his personal contribution to his art.

It has become trite to echo his own statement that he was 'born out of his due time,' still more so to labour the point that he was one of the Pre-Raphaelite nest of singing birds; no English poet of the front

[1] *Life*. Mackail, i. 132.

rank yields less from a study of mere technique. The value of all poets depends not on their literary pedigree but upon their literary progeny. Whether a poet is derivative or self-made is of secondary importance to what he has done. Morris did much. He is a major poet in bulk and parts. He sang songs, like those of his early period which have about them 'a fugitive and haunting scent, or the vague trouble of a dream remembered in a dream,'[1] such as *Two Red Roses across the Moon*, *Near Avalon*, *The Blue Closet* and *Golden Wings*, and at the other extreme, full-blooded stuff like *Sir Giles War-Song*, all master-pieces and all in his first book, which contained in addition those dramatic gems *The Defence of Guenevere*; *Sir Peter Harpdon's End* and *King Arthur's Tomb*. He next adventured into more heroic realms with *Jason* and *The Earthly Paradise*, until the same orderly progress which marked the pattern of his whole life evolved the masterly epic, *Sigurd the Volsung*. In addition came his translations of the *Æneids* of Virgil, the *Odyssey* of Homer, and the stories from Scandinavian mythology translated in collaboration with Eiríkr Magnússon; and last of all, the eight long prose romances beginning with *The House of the Wolfings* (1888) and continuing throughout the remainder of his days until the series closed with *The Sundering Flood* in the year of his death.

One of the truest comments upon his poetry comes from his painter-friend Burne Jones, and

[1] *Life*. Mackail, i. 134.

incidentally these comments apply equally to the prose:

'His line is so simple, unencumbered and straight-forward, it endures for ever, conveys its meaning and makes its mark at once. But you cannot find short quotations in him, he must be taken in great gulps. Chaucer is very much the same sort of person as Morris; unless he can begin his tale at the beginning and go on steadily to the end, he's bothered. There is no ingenuity in either of them; the value of their work comes from the extreme simplicity and beautiful directness of their natures. They are neither of them typical artists – typical poets but not typical artists.'[1]

Morris is only a typical poetic artist as he is a typical decorative artist. His poems and romances are verbal tapestries or mural paintings; they have the same leisurely movement, the same quality of design, the same long-windedness and the same meandering charm. He loved the moving pageantry of life, especially of the imaginative life which filled his dreams, and to express this passion he wove words into moving tapestries. A definite sentiment per-vades them, but it is hardly more possible to quote from it than to extract the sentiment out of the Bayeux tapestry. But you can segregate details and those details are invariably pictorial or decorative. Perhaps Morris gave up painting pictures because he

[1] *Memorials of Edward Burne-Jones.* ii. 265.

found he could be more pictorial with words than pigments.

Proof of this is found practically on many pages of his work. His palette is limited to the bright hues of heraldry, and his early poems have the severe outline and sharp formality of the heraldic convention. It is a curious fact also that although he is fond of grey, especially for landscapes, and the eyes of women and men, indefinite shades are rarely described but referred to mysteriously as 'such dyes not known on earth' or 'many unnamed colours.' He has a passion for gold. It is almost impossible to open a page without finding gold in more senses than one. Sometimes the word comes into his titles, 'Golden Wings' and 'Goldilocks and Goldilocks,' but generally it is reserved for internal decorative effect as dominant note in his heraldic design, as in 'Welland River:'

> *For every day that passes by*
> *I wax both pale and green,*
> *From gold to gold of my girdle*
> *There is an inch between.*

or from a more famous and even more heraldic poem:

> *You scarce could see for the scarlet and blue,*
> *A golden helm or a golden shoe;*
> *So he cried, as the fight grey thick at the noon,*
> Two red roses across the moon!

Both *The Earthly Paradise* and *Jason* glitter and

glow with patterns in which gold predominates, there are ships and palaces of gold, and golden banners and keys and doors, golden goddesses and golden hair and the Golden Fleece itself. Sometimes the word lights up a verse like a lamp or as *or* among the *gules* and *azure* light up a shield or a painted window:

In one quick glance these things his eyes did see,
But speedily they turned round to behold
Another sight, for throned on ivory
There sat a woman, whose wet tresses rolled
On to the floor in waves of gleaming gold,
Cast back from such a form as, erewhile shown
To one poor shepherd, lighted up Troy town.

Naked she was, the kisses of her feet
Upon the floor a dying path had made
From the full bath unto her ivory seat;
In her right hand, upon her bosom laid,
She held a golden comb, a mirror weighed
Her left hand down, aback her fair head lay
Dreaming awake of some long vanquished day.[1]

And here is a typical little picture from *Jason*:

But midst there a glittering roof of gold
Thin shafts of pale blue marble did uphold,
And under it, made by the art divine
Of some dead man, before a well-wrought shrine,
Watching her altar, kind and satisfied
The Golden Goddess stood all open-eyed:

[1] 'The Lady of the Land,' in *The Earthly Paradise*.

And round her temple was a little close
Shut by a gilded trellis of red rose
From off the forest green-sward. . . .

This richness of colouring is carried even into northern scene of the magnificent and austere *Sigurd* which opens with a golden couplet:

There was a dwelling of Kings ere the world was
*   waxen old;*
Dukes were the door-wards there, and the roofs were
*   thatched with gold.*

There are those who consider this wealth of imagery a blemish upon the poetry of Morris, and so it would be if there were too much of it or nothing else. But although his pictures have a tendency to approximate to the static condition of tapestries they are part of a movement which is often tempestuous and sometimes violent. His poetic tales are genuine stories with a definite plot. Indeed, they are more than that; they are the finest stories in the world selected for retelling from among those treasuries of the ancient world which 'half as old as time' seem to have conquered time. That they survive translating into a new poetry and move swiftly enough for narrative purposes despite their repeated tendency to linger by the way admiring the beauty of the scenery, is a tribute to the supremacy of William Morris's art. But all such criticisms pass away at the opening of *Sigurd*. Here Morris becomes master of the craft of narrative poetry, for here he succeeds in merging description and narration into a dramatic unity such as we find only in the great epics of Homer, Dante and Milton with whom Morris stands by virtue of this poem.

His prose romances have the same leisurely sweep and theme. They are full of life and movement and the life is always pictorial and the movement stately. The scene is generally the English countryside unspoilt by commerce or 'progress,' and nowhere else may be found descriptions of our rural loveliness at once so clear-cut or so affectionately drawn. This love of earth and particularly of the English earth and its sights and sounds pervades the whole of Morris's poetry as well as his prose, and helps to keep it human. In his prose romances it forms a familiar and friendly background for adventures and incidents, and even people which are of the very stuff which dreams are made of and only become realities by the ease and friendliness of Morris's story-telling. At the same time and in spite of frequent gestures of interest in the reader these long tales which wind and roll like the English road possess a remoteness as though the author were telling them to himself. This combination of reality and romance is characteristic of the man and his approach to life. His craft-work was the result of his desire for better workmanship and design in common utensils and domestic buildings, and his literary work also took the form of protest against unpleasing realities, not only in his polemical writing, but in that extension of the real into the glorified unreal which is so characteristic in his poetic and prose tales. Something real always starts him off on some romantic adventure. Kelmscott Manor House in its summer beauty set him off to Utopia in *News from Nowhere*, and on the title page of *The Roots of the Mountains* a preface in verse indicates that this story, like 'The Hall in the Wood,' was suggested by a passing glimpse of country life 'whiles carried o'er the iron road.'

Morris would seem always to be stretching out his hand to arrest the passing of beautiful things by time or vandalism. He is acutely conscious of the evanescence of life and his poetry and prose are pervaded with a sense of 'quick-coming death.' He looks wistfully at all beautiful things because he knows they will pass away and his passions are roused against those who would destroy or limit our enjoyment of them. He knows also, but is not made less wistful thereby, that bliss is deepened and sharpened by the thought of death:

> *Ah, what begatteth all this storm of bliss*
> *But Death himself, who crying solemnly,*
> *E'en from the heart of sweet Forgetfulness,*
> *Bids us 'Rejoice,' lest pleasureless ye die,*
> *Within a little time must ye go by.*
> *Stretch forth your open hands, and while ye live*
> *Take all the gifts that Death and Life may give.*[1]

Consciousness of death rather than fear of death is the motive of Morris's poetry, and although his

[1] *The Earthly Paradise.* 'March.'

characters sometimes express fear, as when Helen is arming Paris:

> *I grow afraid of death:*
> *The Gods are all against us* . . .[1]

they more often express dissatisfaction and show a desire to make the best of life while opportunity is theirs.

But side by side with this Hedonism, Morris was cultivating a new attitude towards life from his contact with the north and its heroic myths, and gradually this new attitude grew and there is little doubt that had he lived it would have dominated his work. Walter Crane once heard him say that the thought of death did not trouble him, and that 'Life was quite enough';[2] but all the evidence of his art points the other way. Morris was not afraid of death but he was troubled by death, and his poems are very largely consolatory. The very fact that in the prefatory verses to *The Earthly Paradise* he pleads:

> *Of Heaven or Hell I have no power to sing,*
> *I cannot ease the burden of your fears,*
> *Or make quick-coming death a little thing* . . .

is evidence of this trouble, and it would seem that as time passed he found that the æsthetic compromise was not enough, and that a new strength, more austere and more courageous, was needed. This he found in the attitude towards life and death of the

---

[1] *Jason.*
[2] *An Artist's Reminiscences.* 1907. 439.

heroes of the northern legends, and in some lines addressed to an Icelandic tale-teller, quoted from an unpublished MS. by Mackail,[1] he emphasizes his new need:

> *Thou and they brethren sure did gain*
> *That thing for which I long in vain,*
> *The spell, whereby the mist of fear*
> *Was melted, and your ears might hear*
> *Earth's voices as they are indeed.*
> *Well ye have helped me in my need!*

But he feels a kinship with the saga-teller in that he also has used his art to reduce somewhat the evanescence of earthly life, if only by making tales:

> *Made shadows breathe, quickened the dead,*
> *And knew what silent months once said,*
> *Till with the life his life might give*
> *There lived again, and yet shall live.*[2]

William Morris never lacked courage although he always needed consolation. It was his peculiar and admirable distinction to refuse that consolation on any other terms than those which he could apply to all. 'To know that men lived and worked mightily before you is an incentive for you to work faithfully now, that you may leave something to those who come after you.' These words from one of the most inspiring of his addresses,[3] are an epitome of his faith

---

[1] *Life*, i. 263.   [2] *Id.* i. 263.
[3] *Art and the Beauty of the Earth.* 1881.

in art and slightly paraphrased they may be made to express his deeper faith in life and his attitude towards death. To know that men were brave before you is an incentive for you to be brave now, that you may leave your courage to those who come after you.

CHAPTER FOURTEEN

What he Achieved

*

WILLIAM MORRIS was largely a man of affairs, or perhaps better, an artist of affairs, and his belief in the necessity of a more definite and practical relationship between the artist and the artificer was the moving force of his large energies and varied activities. His life-work was an attempt to bring about such an alliance, and if he did not succeed, he set an example which has definitely and beneficially affected both the craftsmanship and the decorative sense of the age. The Morris style of decoration may have disappeared or become degraded, but the idea of good workmanship which William Morris found almost extinct and into which he blew the breath of life still inspires craftsmen in all parts of the world; and, in spite of changes in taste and fashion, and in spite of new theories and newer arts, the better taste in the decorative arts and the closer association between quality of material and suitability of design, which do actually exist even in the commercially minded age which he failed to overthrow, are due almost entirely to his practical enthusiasm for principles which were in the main fundamentally sound.

His central idea is design: design in art as a means towards design in life. Craftsmen in other ages had, of course, been inspired by the underlying principle of design even as Morris understood it, and the study of the art of those ages had helped him in the formulation of his own principles; but, in the past, sense

148

of design as well as sense of proportion were un-
conscious. They were habitual in craftsmanship and
the rule rather than the exception in common things
as well as in those less common things which are now
called works of art.

With Morris design was self-conscious, and
although it sprang, as it should do, and as it does in
the best craftsmanship, out of the nature and quality
of the materials used with due regard for their
purpose, what he called 'eventfulness of form,' it
suffered from the circumstances governing its birth.
We know that Morris came to make beautiful things
as a protest against the predominance of ugly things,
and although the quality of his craftsmanship is in-
contestable it often lacks that inevitability of design
which is the mark of a passion for expression rather
than a zeal for reform. Beautiful as his creations are,
their beauty is obviously and ineradically the outcome of workmanship performed laboriously and
immaculately in a dead language; and, if that workmanship was not wholly moved by principle (Morris
was too much of an artist for that), the pressure of
principle was sufficient to give most of it a significance other than that necessary to inevitable art.

Morris recognized the importance of design in
medieval craftsmanship at an early stage; it appealed
to him naturally as a youth, and he would devote long
hours to the study of it. But it was Ruskin's theory
of Gothic which ultimately formed his mind and
taught him to consider the inner and moral as
distinct from the æsthetic meaning of the fine crafts-

manship of the past. He believed with Ruskin that
excellence in craftsmanship could only be the result
of human labour joyfully performed; and he admitted his continued discipleship by printing on
the Kelmscott Press, *Unto this Last* and *The Nature
of Gothic*, the two works which profoundly affected
his outlook upon art and life. These works were
Morris's inspiration and his undoing. Without
them, it is true, he might have become a priest; but
with them he risked his immortal soul as an artist by
becoming a reformer. He sold all that he had and
gave to the poor – often, those most hopeless of all
poor folk, the poor of spirit. But he was too big to be
wholly exterminated even by his own teaching, let
alone by his master's. William Morris succeeded in
escaping from the fulness of the Ruskinian doctrine
of art by approximating more and more to the condition of the great craftsmen, not of the Middle
Ages, but of that Italian Renaissance which was
from Ruskin's point of view little more than a
Gotterdammerung. The spiritual kin of William
Morris were Michael Angelo, Leonardo da Vinci
and Benvenuto Cellini, not the anonymous craft-
masters of the Medieval Guilds.

Ruskin was always a medievalist, Morris was a
modernist. Ruskin would have, with certain modi-
fications, restored the past; he stated, quite clearly,
in the book he described as 'the truest, rightest
worded, and most serviceable' he had written, that
he was not a Socialist but a Tory of the old school,
although, later in life, he modified this view. Morris

just as frankly looked to the future and announced himself a Socialist. The past for him was merely the starting-place for Utopia.

Morris would go back for the purpose of picking up a lost tradition of good workmanship; from thence he would move forwards. With the help of Ruskin he found this good workmanship in the Middle Ages, when the Craft Guild was at the height of its powers. Surviving articles of that period have about them an organic charm combined with utility which have only been attained on few occasions since the break-up of the Guild system. Morris asked himself why these articles were so much more beautiful and so much more durable than similar products of our own time; the answer was that these things were produced for excellence and durability rather than for immediate financial gain; and, further, that they were produced by men who were not only familiar, in many instances, with the ultimate users of their products, but who had been trained in the making of complete articles, rather than in that specialization upon the separate parts of an article, which modern industrial methods have made inevitable.

Morris devoted his life to what may be called architechtonic and local as distinct from individual and universal craftsmanship. He started the workshops at Merton Abbey and Queen Square and the shop in Oxford Street for this purpose, and his fabrics, tapestries, and chintzes, his wallpapers, his stained glass, and his printing became the emblems and inspirations of fine workmanship all the world over. The result of his effort was surprising and not without irony. His aim was to make what he was fond of calling 'useful pieces of goods' under conditions which would insure that they were also works of art, and that these products of a new-old method should be generally accessible for common usage. But he had reckoned without his host, for when he had created his beautiful things, only the rich could buy them.

But irony had reserved her master-stroke for the anti-climax. The beautiful pieces of goods made under conditions of joyful labour for ultimate common usage by the Socialist-craftsman, not only became the special totems and phylacteries of the plutocrat and the poseur, but these inimitable goods proved to be imitable in the worst sense of the word. They became a fashion. Their superficial appearance was copied and marketed as the new art. Morris became the *dernier cri* like a frock or a hat. He was reproduced like 'period' furniture. Art became a *vogue* and the word 'artistic' competed for a little while with the moral pre-eminence of 'respectable.' Art, in short, in Whister's acid phrase, was 'upon the town.' It was even worse than that, it was in the schools. Young ladies and ladies of riper years abandoned their needles for pokers. The Morris 'note' appeared in poker-work. Copper was beaten into deliberately crude decorations with the hammer-work ostentatiously left in to show that it was hand-made. The Morris style was vulgarized and debased until it became a by-word and a reproach where it ought to have been a shield and an inspiration.

He wanted beautiful things for himself, and he was so constituted that he wanted others to have them, for he knew that such things were not only beautiful to look upon and pleasant to use, but he believed also that in the creation of them men had been happy, and he wanted all men to be happy. It is here that a fundamental departure from the teaching of his master may be noted. Morris was opposed to the idea of art for art's sake, but he was a believer in happiness. Ruskin on the other hand, although the apostle of the gospel of joy in work, looked upon good work as the object of joy and not upon joy as a thing in itself. Ruskin was a puritan and a moralist with Spartan tendencies a little the worse for wear, but Morris was a frank Hedonist saved from preciosity by sheer love of life. He demanded that all things made by men should be the symbols of joyful work, because happiness was a desirable thing in itself. Fine craftsmanship was desirable because it was a promoter of happiness both in procedure and the results of that procedure. And it was because our present methods of commerce made it impossible to practise such craftsmanship that, as I have already shown, he came to be a Socialist.

Morris was a practical visionary; and if he never reached his goal it was not because he lacked energy or the capacity for work, but because either the times were not ripe or there was something inherently impossible in his dream: probably a little of

each. Certainly the times were not ripe, and the
poet-craftsman himself grew to feel that a practical
Socialism could scarcely be made of existing human
material. He even grew hopeless about his fellow
propagandists, particularly those who did not adopt
his enthusiasm for the crafts.

But the real check to his dream was the mechanical
industry which he opposed. He realized well enough
that modern commercial production had evolved a
machine which callously used might and did evoke
disastrous evil; he did not realize that not only had
that machine conquered the world, but that rightly,
humanly, and imaginatively used, it might remould
our chaotic industrial system if not nearer to his ideal
of joyful craftsmanship, at least a little nearer to his
imagined realm of cleanliness and seemly leisure.
Indeed with the sure intuition of the poet, as far back
as the early eighteen-eighties, he saw that 'the day of
the organization of man is dawning'; and if he would
have organized differently from what has now become possible and imperative, the germ of this new
idea was in him, even if we do not know how he
would have worked it out.

Two, at least, of his claims have been admitted in
principle; one, that labour should have a greater
share in the rewards of production; two, that there
can be no happiness in work unless those who labour
should take a human interest in the things they do.
True, he preached against control, and himself
could not and would not suffer it; but that was
because he was essentially a master-man and

necessarily an autocrat (no matter how benevolent) in his own workshops. He would have things done his own way, which happened to be the great way, and there are many still living who recall his picturesque rage when designs went wrong and workmanship fell below the level he had set. It should also be remembered that he approved of the organization of the Craft Guilds with their grades of Master, Journeyman, and Apprentice. Morris was no leveller of personality or power; equality for him was equality of opportunity and of access to the necessities of life. His democratic faith assumed inherent if not always evident goodwill in his fellows, which could be awakened into a preference for good work rather than bad, and fairness and generosity of behaviour rather than petty tyranny and meanness.

He practised what he preached. Early and late his great energies were devoted to hammering out, without concession to popular or accepted taste, an exalted ideal. He was no mere failure or congenital grumbler. A big fellow in every way, he lived and worked joyously, disinterestedly, and wholesomely, and, if he did not alter the factory system which he loathed, he left an example of good workmanship which is practical in its ultimate idea, if not always in its immediate method.

There was a far-seeing sanity about his attitude towards workmanship. Strip away his æsthetics, forget his poetry, if you can; scrap even his Socialism, there will yet remain a practical vision of sane labour which is economically as well as morally sound, and which, rightly understood, should be a tonic for our own time and an inspiration for times yet to be. For whether art be the expression of man's joy in his work or not, and whatever else it may be, it most certainly is not solely that, the inauguration of an era of joyful labour is the most urgent need of a bewildered and hag-ridden world; and the combination of that joyous work with fellowship and the cultivation of simple but exquisite tastes a most desirable ideal.

There will always be a demand for personality in production, and, as culture develops, that demand will grow, side by side with the better organization of the impersonal production of those goods and machines which are inherently standardizable. But there is no final reason why the craftsman who tends a machine should not have as much joy in his work as the craftsman who creates by hand.

William Morris confused the issues between design and decoration. He did not sufficiently differentiate. Decoration for him was the added touch given to a piece of goods by art; design was the true proportion of the goods in reference to purpose. The two in his philosophy should go together. But that is not essential. Design in the last resort is fitness: and fitness should be signified by form without exterior or added decoration; eventfulness and fitness of form should coincide.

With all his reverence for the past Morris was not blind to the possibilities of a new art. Perhaps he felt that civilization had gone too far ever to retrieve

its lost simplicity. 'Yet,' he said, in a lecture delivered at the London Institution, in 1880, 'the new
art may yet arise among us, and even if it have the
hands of a child together with the heart of a troubled
man, still it may bear on for us to better times the
tokens of our reverence for the Life of Man upon
the Earth.' This new art would be the outcome of
a regained simplicity made possible by earnest practice of the art of doing without useless so-called
comforts and luxuries. 'Learn to do without,' he
preached in the same lecture; 'there is virtue in those
words; a force that rightly used would choke both
demand and supply of Mechanical Toil: would make
it stick to its last: the making of machines. And
then from simplicity of life would rise up the longing
for beauty, which cannot yet be dead in men's souls,
and we know that nothing can satisfy that demand
but Intelligent work rising gradually into Imaginative work; which will turn all "operatives" into
workmen, into artists, into men.'[1] So far as we can
see this dream of Morris is farther away than ever,
and although the 'operative' may be having a better
time of it, he is certainly not any more of an artist
than he was, nor is there any evidence that he wants
to be.

It is conceivable, however, that a man working
under conditions of fitness with regard to time,
housing and reward, and who is keen about the final
fitness of the thing he makes, whether he be responsible for the whole or only a part of it, will experience

[1] *Hopes and Fears for Art.* 215–217.

that joy in his work, and become that dignified and healthy being which both Ruskin and Morris imagined. In any event a joyous consciousness of the new mechanical conditions must be evolved, for however the smaller handicrafts may thrive in the future, they can never supplant the factory with its eternal miracle of machinery and its unimagined vistas of productiveness.

For the rest in so far as he was an artist he will remain for a delight to our own generation and to generations to come. It is again ironic that he was most an artist in the thing he did most easily and regarded as a by-product: his poetry. Whatever happens to his furniture and his tapestries, his stained glass and his printing, his poetry will live on increasing and multiplying its appreciators, because at its best it is poetry and nothing else, content with its own loveliness. And as the years pass future generations may inquire about the poet himself and they will learn that William Morris who sang these deathless songs was also a good citizen; and that he worked always in the public interest, and strove to realize a noble ideal by the personal example of tireless industry and good workmanship.

BIBLIOGRAPHY

Works of William Morris

The Collected Works of William Morris, edited by May Morris, are published by Messrs. Longmans, Green & Co. in 24 volumes. These volumes are not sold separately, but all the principal works are accessible in various forms, many in popular reprints.

Biographical, Critical, and Bibliographical Studies

The Art of William Morris. By Aymer Vallance. 1897.

The Books of William Morris described, with some account of his doings in Literature and the Allied Arts. By H. Buxton Forman. 1897.

A Bibliography of the Works of William Morris. By Temple Scott. 1897.

The Life of William Morris. By J. W. Mackail. 2 vols. 1899.

Morris as Workmaster. By W. R. Lethaby. 1901.

William Morris: Poet, Craftsman, Socialist. By E. L. Cary. 1902.

William Morris: Craftsman – Socialist. By Holbrook Jackson. 1908.

William Morris. By Alfred Noyes. 1908.

William Morris. By John Drinkwater. 1912.

The First Morris: Primitæ. By Dixon Scott. 1912.

William Morris and the Communist Ideal. (Fabian Tract, 167.) By Mrs. Townshend. 1912.

William Morris. By A. Compton-Rickett. 1913.

William Morris: His Work and Influence. By A. Clutton-Brock. 1914.

William Morris and the Early Days of the Socialist
Movement. By J. Bruce Glasier, with a Preface
by May Morris. 1921.
The Kelmscott Press and William Morris. By H.
Halliday Sparling. 1924.
William Morris and his Poetry. By B. Ifor Evans.
1925.

Works Containing References to William Morris

Letters of Dante Gabriel Rossetti to William Alling-
ham, 1854–1870. Edited by George Birkbeck
Hill. 1897.
The Memorials of Edward Burne-Jones. By G.
B.-J. [Lady Burne-Jones.] 2 vols. 1904.
An Artist's Reminiscences. By Walter Crane. 1907.
Old Familiar Faces. By Theodore Watts-Dunton.
1916.
Letters of Algernon Charles Swinburne, with some
Personal Recollections. By Thomas Hake and
Arthur Compton-Rickett. 1918.
My Diaries. By Wilfrid Scawen Blunt. 2 vols.
1921.
The Eighteen-Nineties. By Holbrook Jackson.
1923.